Dead
Bees
Still
Sting

Susan Cormier

Dead Bees Still Sting

Tales of Life at the Edge of Nature

GREYSTONE BOOKS

Vancouver/Berkeley/London

Copyright © 2026 by Susan Cormier

26 27 28 29 30   5 4 3 2 1

The publisher expressly prohibits the use of *Dead Bees Still Sting* in connection with the development of any software program, including, without limitation, training a machine learning or generative artificial intelligence (AI) system.

All rights reserved, including those for text and data mining, AI training, and similar technologies. No part of this book may be reproduced, stored in a retrieval system, or transmitted, in any form or by any means, without the prior written consent of the publisher or a license from The Canadian Copyright Licensing Agency (Access Copyright). For a copyright license, visit accesscopyright.ca or call toll free to 1-800-893-5777.

Greystone Books Ltd.
greystonebooks.com

This book includes descriptions of situations that may be dangerous. The author and the publisher accept no liability for any damages arising as a result of the direct or indirect application of any element of the contents of this book.

Cataloguing data available from Library and Archives Canada
ISBN 978-1-77840-201-2 (pbk.)
ISBN 978-1-77840-202-9 (epub)

Developmental editing by Jennifer Croll
Stylistic editing by Holly Vestad
Proofreading by Lisa Frenette
Cover design by DSGN Dept.
Cover illustration by Elena Bragina/iStock (blackberries);
Olesya Frolova/iStock (bee)
Text design by Fiona Siu

Printed and bound in Canada on FSC® certified paper at Friesens. The FSC® label means that materials used for the product have been responsibly sourced.

Greystone Books thanks the Canada Council for the Arts, the British Columbia Arts Council, the Province of British Columbia through the Book Publishing Tax Credit, and the Government of Canada for supporting our publishing activities.

EU Safety Information: Easy Access System Europe, Mustamäe tee 50, 10621 Tallinn, Estonia, gpsr.requests@easproject.com.

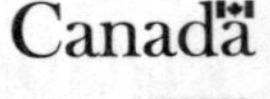

Greystone Books gratefully acknowledges the xʷməθkʷəy̓əm (Musqueam), Sḵwx̱wú7mesh (Squamish), and səlilwətaɬ (Tsleil-Waututh) peoples on whose land our Vancouver head office is located.

Contents

the future rushes toward us
    like a heat wave, a tidal wave, a wave
        of industrial seduction, the destruction
of ecology. and we
    are breathing in this
        thin mist of existence, subsisting upon faith
    and humanity

THERE ARE OVER twenty thousand species of bees in the world. Except where otherwise stated, all mentions of bees in this book refer to *Apis mellifera*, the Western honey bee.

Storm

I RETURN FROM A road trip, just in time for the windstorms. It happens every spring: The cold and warm air currents of this tilting planet clash over the ocean and send furious gusts inland, marking the shift in season with storms punctuated by random power outages and the occasional afternoon of torrential rain.

Inside the house, my suitcase lies abandoned on the living room floor, stuffed with dusty clothes and a dog-eared journal of scribbled, dozy road dreams. The indoor pets sniff at it, trying to decipher the strange smells and the stories behind them. I'll unpack it all later. For now, I have more important things to do: a covered porch to stand on, a storm to watch.

HOW TO WATCH A STORM

FACE INTO THE wind with your glasses on. If you turn your head sideways, the wind will blow pine needles and dirt into your eyes. If you put your back to it, your hair will lash your face, and you will not see any falling tree or spinning branch as it plummets toward you. Face into the wind; it is safest.

Remember your childhood, storms on the lake. Your mother would wake you at odd hours, urging you to "put your coat and boots on, quickly, you need to come see." The waves smashing into the shore. She'd warn you to stand on the open rocks, away from the trees. "The falling branches are dangerous," she'd say. Lightning may strike. Stand in the open, on the bare rocks, and watch the water rage.

There are no rocks here, no open shoreline, just a covered porch and trees too far away to harm you. But the dry pine needles spin like sharp snowflakes, and the branches crack and rattle like ambushing soldiers. The wind comes from the southeast, but if it were to shift or ricochet off the mountains and come back from behind you, there are trees on the other side of the house, close enough and tall enough to be fatal. Stand with your face in the wind and your ears cocked like a rabbit's, listening, always listening, for the crack and creak and rattle of falling trees.

Do not mistake the occasional gunshot sounds for danger. They are distant electricity. They are transformers rupturing, dropping neighborhoods into cold and darkness. They are power lines snapping, flailing like enraged octopuses that charge the contacted ground into electrified danger. But they are not on your street. You are safe, relatively, to stand on the porch and watch the world explode.

THE WINDSTORMS SEEM more violent now than in previous years—but is that due to changes in global weather patterns, or is this little acreage just more exposed and vulnerable since the neighbors cut down all their sturdy pine trees and the municipality bulldozed the ninety-acre forest at the back of the property?

Until recent years, there were more trees, the view across the neighboring properties was short and blocked, and behind us was a great forest. Now, much of the wilderness has been cleared away in early preparation for the demolition and removal of all that is here. The city an hour away is growing, its limbs of development stretching to land where I stand. Now, the lawns are riddled with thick stumps, the line of sight stretches several hundred yards, and only a thin belt of untouched, wild trees frames the back end of this row of houses. A single, massive, older-growth ponderosa pine stretches high above its arboreal companions, ancient and dry, the proud, old monarch of a shrinking kingdom.

Loose leaves press into piles against the garage, the workshop, the beehives. The gate to the dog's yard rattles and bangs a metallic staccato. The tire swing, a worn souvenir of long-grown children, twists and spins. Beneath the clack of swaying tree trunks banging against each other, the rattle of broken, fallen branches and random objects blowing about, and the monstrous howl of wind, the world is surprisingly uninhabited, quiet.

The wild cottontail rabbits that graze on our lawn are absent, hiding under porches and bushes, waiting for the chaos to pass. The predatory wild animals are also out of sight: The coyotes have no prey to chase, and the hawks and eagles are unwilling to try to battle the wind with their wings. Our bird feeders spin and flip and crash to the ground, spilling their seeds across the lawn, their usual menagerie of patrons—finches, robins, chickadees, assorted boring brown birds—huddling somewhere in the trees instead of filling the air with their wings and a symphony of assorted songs. Even the squirrels and crows do not come in for their daily feast of peanuts and food scraps. One would think that at least the frogs would be extra loud in their anticipation of rain and puddles and post-storm bugs: but no, they, too, are silent, self-protectively hiding, unaware of the future.

My little quails are huddled at the back of their pen, bright eyes wide, secure and safe against the blast of prickly pine needles but nevertheless alarmed by the noise and upheaval. Today, at least, they will not be bothered by hungry rats tunneling under their home or trying to chew through the pen's wired walls. Our honey bees are fine, snuggled into their sturdy hives waiting for calm and sunshine. The wind here, though dramatic, is not strong enough to knock their multi-hundred-pound homes over. If we lived in another region, I'd have to venture beyond the safety of the porch and frantically ratchet the hives down with thick vinyl straps, pile cement bricks on their roofs, and hope for the best.

Inside the house, the pets abandon their perusal of my travel luggage, distracted by the flickering lights and external cacophony. The dog paces the hallway, seeking refuge from the howl of the wind in the eaves and, finding none, curls up in his soft bed with his nose on his paws. The cat sits in the window watching unfamiliar objects blow by, alternately staring silently and loudly inventing new vowels.

Down the road, one of the neighbors has foolishly taken to flying a kite, forgetting that the momentary absence of rain does not mean the absence of possible lightning strikes.

I squint at our apple trees, trying to see if they have begun to sprout blossoms. Heavy wind during a bloom can make for a sad harvest: torn of their soft petals, tiny flowers lose their ability to attract the pollinators that will fertilize them and initiate the process of forming fruit.

A deep *crack* thuds into my ears, and I glance back up to the fringe of swaying forest. The crown of the tall monarch tree has broken, sheared off in the fierce wind. The massive treetop falls, crashing across the neighbor's workshop and garden. The neighbor reels in his frantically twisting kite and runs into his house.

<hr>

NATURE CULLS THE weak and the vulnerable through massive destruction, disease, the fury of the weather, an upheaval of stasis, leaving only the strong, the healthy, the protected to carry on a species' genes. The dodo bird, isolated on an island without predators, lost its ability to defend itself. A small dog, shaped by generations of breeding and domestic comfort, forgets how to hunt. A tree unaccustomed to wind has a weak trunk.

We wait for stability, for the disruptions to end—in nature, in our lives, in our human-built global systems—but that will never come. The act of existing is chaotic.

We are afraid of change, because we inherently fear that which is different and unfamiliar. This fear has kept us alive for millennia. Back when we were wilder animals, creeping through forests and across plains, we evolved to avoid the strange and the unknown. Those who bravely tasted the unfamiliar berries or ventured into unexplored spaces often ended up poisoned, attacked, or killed. The cautious ones who stayed close to home and feasted on known foods were more likely to survive, breed, and create new generations of timid beings. Many baby rabbits are very bold and courageous, and they may approach and sniff an outstretched hand. Many baby rabbits die. The most skittish wild rabbits live longest. And so, we evolved to fear that which we do not know.

The presence of fear does not definitively indicate the presence of danger. Fear alerts us to the *possibility* of danger, the need for caution.

We stand like deer in this Anthropocene, ears cocked toward the horizon. The storm brews around us—the air is electric, the sky greengray and moving.

Deer do not run from a storm. They do not hide between the trees and in the brambles. They sleep in fields and long-grassed open spaces where they are safest—they can see around them, watch for predators, rest safely as the rain falls and the sky falls and the trees fall.

When the wind calms and the sky clears, the world will be different. Trees will have fallen. New ones will grow in their place. The earth will be washed, sloughed off into thick, muddy piles. It will dry and form a new landscape. There will be injuries. There will be some dead. The deer and the rabbits will rise from their beds and feed again, be fed upon. There will be change.

THE WIND MELLOWS and gives way to rain as the air dims into dusk and the western sky flares into a bright, fiery sunset.

Soundlessly, the porch light goes out, and the neighbors' windows go dark. Power outage: from a torn power line, exploded transformer, or fallen branches landing on wires somewhere. Given the extent of damage such storms create, and the limited workforce of municipal labour crews, the power could be out for a few hours or for days. Likely, our house will remain dark until B returns from work and starts our generator. The backyard will be filled with the low grumbling, chugging thunder of an obnoxious, gas-powered machine; in the cold and rainy darkness, there will be at least one house that has warmth, quiet shelter, and windows full of light. And tomorrow, if the weather is calm, there will be fallen branches to gather and pile up to burn, blown-about broken things to retrieve and repair, and a garden, beehives, and quails to check on and attend.

The sunset swells, then retreats and disappears. The rain slows, then stops. In the new, quiet darkness, eaves troughs and branches drip, and the frogs begin to sing. Beyond the beehives and quail pen, beyond the fringe of forest trees, beyond the farmlands and fields and picket fence–cut forests, the distant horizon glows with the steady orange haze of the encroaching metropolis.

PART 1

Spring

THE LIVING ROOM fills with a metallic clatter, the sound of machine guns. I trace the source to the gas fireplace, up the pipe, and out onto the roof. Perched on the chimney is a crimson-garbed woodpecker with puffed chest and bright eyes, drumming enthusiastically on the metal chimney to attract a ladyfriend. Perhaps this technique works, but I wouldn't encourage the males of my species to follow suit lest they get kicked out of bars and libraries.

Advice to a
New Beekeeper

DO NOT KEEP bees.

Keep cattle, or chickens, or dogs. Their emotions are recognizable, their ailments familiar. Their speech, though foreign, is in a language we understand.

A FRAME OF honeycomb slips from your hands, cracks against the hive edge, and tumbles to the ground. A dark storm of bees roars up and around you.

A hundred stings at once is an emergency. A thousand, a death sentence. A hive contains thirty-five thousand to sixty-five thousand bees.

Stand still, contrite and breathing, surrounded by a dark hurricane, untouched, waiting.

A HIVE IS a galaxy, an ever-turning sphere.

The queen lays her eggs, a thousand a day, one per honeycomb cell, spiraling outward from the center of the hive, precise and methodical. Each day she continues without reprieve, spiraling ever outward, forming a broodball of offspring, the eldest in the middle, ever moving.

The eggs are near-invisible white slivers. Follow the spiral back down into the broodball and see curled, hatched larvae, then their older siblings growing long and plump, then the eldest brood sealed shut in their wax cradles for pupation. As the young bees emerge from their cells, chewing through the wax lids and squeezing out like damp kittens with ruffled fur, a circle of newly emptied cells forms. The queen circles back and continues, one egg per reused cell, working at the heels of her eldest brood as they emerge, spiraling outward, ever outward.

***

DRINK COLD WATER before working with your beehives. An hour in the hives is three in linear time, and the sun beats down harshly. Time flows in spirals inside honeycomb, and sunlight has never been so heavy.

***

LEARN THE LANGUAGE of bees. There is no lexicon, no dictionary. They speak in song and scent and secrets and dance. The closest similar language is that of trees, octopuses, or a school of fish.

Learn the smell of anger, sharp and thin like spilled bleach. Learn the low, soothing hum of calm and the ramping pitch of outrage. Learn the gentle warmth and sweet air of a balanced colony.

Learn to read the comb like hieroglyphs. The even, smooth cells of a strong nectar harvest. The irregular, patchy pattern of a failing queen. The thick, mottled wax stalactites of an overcrowding hive.

Learn the language. You cannot speak it, but you can listen. Listen with your body.

AT THE OUTER edges of the broodball is a layer of beebread: dry pollen packed tight into cells for feeding the larvae. Young worker bees ferry the bread inward to the babies, nurture the healthy brood, and remove the diseased and deformed. From the outer edge of the broodball, each worker bee walks the radius of the spiral a thousand times a day, carrying food in, carrying the deceased out.

DO NOT FEAR deaths or stings. Both happen frequently. Fear fire, drought; fear dusty, parched earth and scorched, wilting flowers. Fear fire, yet carry one with you, waving smoke like fairy dust, like a priest's incense-filled thurible, quietly chanting blessings and calm.

Do not fear stings or the possibility of them. Carry in your arms a box housing fifty thousand bees and think nothing of it. Place your bare hand softly on two hundred moving bodies at once and know only warmth.

Fear tiny mites, the spread of spores and viruses—watch for twisted wings, spasming bodies, the rotting stench of dying brood.

Fear animals with paws, and hornets. When a small midnight shadow scurries across your lawn, throw rocks, apples, anything at hand, cursing softly to not wake the neighbors. Hiss and growl. Set up traps and hope for the best.

DO NOT TALK much about the males, the drones. They are stupid, simple, and vulnerable. As larvae, their fat torsos ruin your perfect honeycomb; as adults, you notice when they are there or gone but little else. They are fickle and wander from hive to hive, eating food stores and sleeping among strangers. They serve only one purpose: to breed. They are simpleminded, and after achieving their goal, they die dramatically, explosively, plummeting to the earth like proud warriors falling in battle. In the autumn, they are kicked out en masse, vulnerable and hopeless, and die of exposure. Laugh about them or feel sorry for them. They are mostly useless and cannot defend themselves. Love their big, dark eyes, their thick bodies, the way they cling to you when you hold them, unwilling to leave the warmth of your hand.

FORGET THAT YOUR hands are large and clumsy. Move slowly. Breathe easily. The scent of held breath is an alarm bell of danger. Breathe. Be calm.

Some call it poetry, a meditation. Others call it science or art. It is none of these. You are here to work, to lift heaviness as the sun beats your back and head into a thick, pounding ache and the light sparks hot, harsh knives and the sweat denies relief.

You are here to work, to be worked over. And you are a thick, dumb animal of clumsy meat.

GET USED TO the common questions. Answer them at length in thoughtful detail or briefly and inappropriately.

How many bees do you have?
Seven.
Do you make honey?
I tried, but I don't have the right body parts.
Have you ever been stung?

WHEN A HIVE is warm and growing, lean into it. Breathe in the sweet, waxy air deep and slow. Rest your hands on the soft layers of moving bodies. Here, there is only life, hope, and the birthing of ancient religions.

THE MODERN MYTHOLOGY is full of romantic falsehoods. That bees recognize their keepers. That they willingly exchange honey for a home and protection. That they understand your actions. That a spoonful of sugar water left in the yard will help them. That honey cures all ailments. That the profits from selling honey will balance out your labor. That a box of bees in your yard is an easy hobby. That you do this for profits, for honey, for money.

WHEN A HIVE outgrows its confining quarters, the queen and half the bees will swarm, leaving to form a new colony elsewhere. Stand in the sunlight and watch. As the bees fly in widening circles, tens of thousands of them, more bees than you have ever seen in flight at once, watch them.

When they land and form a clump, I cannot advise you, with your bare arms and loose summer clothes, to reach your hand out to the humming, undulating mass. The breeze from their wings is so small and warm. The inside of the swarm is bubbles of champagne, the purring of thousands of kittens. Your skin is surrounded by danger. A hundred stings will land you in the hospital—a thousand will kill. I cannot advise you to do this, to lift your hand into the smallest of heavens.

THE SMALLEST UNIT of measurement is a beespace: the width of a honeycomb cell, the distance between one frame of comb and the next, the smallest entrance opening. Bees measure space by stretching their legs, forming chains, climbing across each other's backs. Two patches of comb built separately then expanded to combine will always meet seamlessly, the hexagon pattern aligning precisely, tiny wax flakes pressed into perfect position.

A colony of honey bees visits two million flowers and flies fifty thousand miles to make one pound of honey. Bees consume nine pounds of honey to make one pound of wax. A single honey bee cannot survive alone, but a colony can build an empire. Harvest comb for wax sparingly, gently, taking only the broken and the discarded and leaving the rest for the bees to reuse.

REIMAGINE LINEAR TIME. A bee lives for a few weeks or months. Each generation builds brood comb for larvae they will never see grown, stores food for future siblings they will never meet, prepares the hive for a winter they will never know. Reimagine generations. A bee lives for a few weeks or months; a queen, for years. She lays hundreds of thousands of eggs, her children growing and dying around her as she circles, spirals, methodically. Reimagine longevity. A bee will create a quarter teaspoon of honey in its entire lifetime. The bee will live a few weeks or months. The honey will remain unspoiled for thousands of years, perhaps eternity. Reimagine goals, your legacies, in this twisting linear time.

Consider a new definition of immortality.

WASH EVERYTHING IN cold water, because heat melts wax into a thick smear that clogs drainpipes. Rinse everything in hot, because the remnants of honey flow slow in cold. Your beekeeping suit heavy with sweat, your casual clothes spattered with honey and wax, your bedsheet grabbed hastily from the linen closet and thrown over a hive to stave off a blitzkrieg of wasps.

Your perfectly polished laminate floors will become speckled with sticky wax bits that gather dust despite the hours you spend scraping them clean with a thumbnail. The dryer filter will grow a fine film of wax. There will be so many things you never thought you'd have to scrub clean. Your home will smell of summer: sweet, bright, the rising scent of warm honey.

———

A COLONY CAN last in perpetuity, each generation bringing in food for its younger siblings, each faltering queen laying the egg of her successor. They are complex and intricate and self-sufficient, but nature is even more so, and unpredictable and cruel. Despite your best efforts, they will die.

Perhaps not this month or next, or this year or next, but eventually, they will die. Of parasites, disease, attack by another colony, starvation, thirst, exposure to pesticides, cold snaps, overheating, natural disasters, poor genetics, wasps, bears, entrapment in the hive, not enough space, or some unknown reason. Yes, they will die.

———

WATCH THE TREES and the skies, head cocked sideways like a rabbit wary of hawks, looking, always looking, for the umber clump of a swarm or the sunlit shooting stars of foraging bees.

———

A DEAD HIVE sounds like motionless wind. It smells like the dark cool of autumn, even in stifling summer heat. You will be quietened, suddenly, by the unexpected silence. You do not need to see: your outstretched hand recognizes the unmoving air, the stillness of a deceased colony; your body knows the musty smell.

———

MASTER THE ART of saving photos for months and then deleting them. If you see the queen, photograph her. She is beautiful and unique. Take photos of perfect capped frames of honey, symmetrical spirals of brood, translucent-white new comb. Their tiny beauty is magnificent. Take photos for reference: *this is disease, this is a swarm in progress, this is a queenless hive.* At the end of the season, review them and remind yourself: *this is unique beauty, this is destruction in progress.*

Forget why you took them. They all look the same, indistinguishable from each other, like newborn babies overdocumented by zealous parents. The queens with their bulbous abdomens, the rows of hexagonal comb, tiny specks of bees against a flat, blue sky. Forget their profundity, the moments. Delete them all.

YOUR FRIENDS WILL misidentify everything bee-like as a honey bee and will turn to you for advice.

They will say, *There are bees in our attic* or *under the dog-house.* Or, *There are bees building a nest in the apple tree. Please come relocate them.* You will arrive with your suit on and gear in hand and will find hornets, paper wasps, bum-blebees. They will ask, *But you'll take care of them, right?*

Tell them this story: *I phone you to say come fetch your dog that is attacking my chickens. You arrive with col-lar and leash and see not your dog but a coyote, wolf, or hyena.* "But you'll take care of it, right?" *I say.*

Your friends will misidentify everything. Ask for photos before you leave your house.

IN THE COLD months, the bees cluster in a sphere within the hive. The queen is at the center, for protection. As the bees on the outside chill, they burrow into the center for warmth. The cluster spirals inward, inward, always inward, a constant spiral of heat and food, the queen at the center like a solar system's star.

Hold your hand to the side of the hive and imagine the sound of warmth. Picture the smell of a spherical galaxy spiraling in mathematical perfection. Are they alive or dead? Schrödinger's hive. Remember hope.

RECONSIDER YOUR UNDERSTANDING of life. A colony of bees being euthanized will scream. Dead bees still sting. Bees have three genders. A single bee cannot survive alone. The mother outlives her children again and again.

A hive with a failed queen dies slowly, population dwindling, the final brood hatch a thick wave of fat drones who abandon their home. The queen dies. The colony dies. The Hail Mary drones, single-minded and suicidal, carry their family's genetics to other queens, other colonies. Reconsider your definition of death. Of persistence. Of survival.

WHEN YOU KNOW the bees' language so well that you smell it in your dreams, compose an answer to that oft-asked question: *If you're not in it for the honey, then why keep bees? With the expense and the backaches and the deaths and the heaviness of heat and the stings—why?*

In the bright midsummer heat, turn your back to the sun and hold a frame of comb to the light. Watch a young bee hatch from its wax cell, turning slowly as it chews its way to freedom, fur ruffled and damp, tiny shoulders pressing and struggling, turning slowly, a spinning single star surrounded by a greater galaxy. Stand still, quiet and breathing, surrounded by a warm hurricane, waiting.

Compose an answer in a language you understand but cannot speak. Hold your thick, clumsy hands in the shape of new wax and a soft, humming song. Measure the distances in beespaces; do not use numbers. Breathe out softly, a spiraling galaxy in constant motion. Dance the language of ancient religions.

Aria

A T NIGHT AND on cooler spring days, I hear him. He has a big voice that carries around the corner of the house, across the yard. Even with the windows shut, I can hear him from inside.

Judging by the volume, I suspect he is quite large, at least the size of my palm. Only a big body would have a voice of such impressive volume. But whenever I try to triangulate his location, he goes silent.

In the late afternoons, he sings over and over, his voice clear and loud. He must be protecting his territory or serenading a mate. But he must also be camouflaged or hidden beneath some object, for he remains unseen. I look behind leaning boards, beneath the porch, under large rocks—nothing. I find only garter snakes, creeping spiders, tiny frogs, creatures that are silent or have tiny voices.

One afternoon, I am standing quietly in my garden, pondering the tangles of vines and leaves, and I hear his call, rich and loud, right behind me. He is in my gardening shed.

I quickly open the door of the shed, listening for the scramble of an animal trying to hide. But there is only silence, the stillness of leaning rakes and shovels.

Carefully, I lift each gardening tool and toss it behind me, watching the floor of the shed for movement. Nothing. I crouch down, run my hands through the scattered gloves and trowels, searching for the source of this big and boisterous voice. But I find only clumps of dirt, dead spiders, an empty seed packet.

I brace my hand against the door to steady myself as I stand—and pause. In a dent on the inside of the door is a tiny green frog, no bigger than the last joint of my thumb. He is motionless, his feet tucked in close, as small as he can make himself, pretending to be invisible. And it occurs to me that the smooth, hollow walls of the gardening shed reflect and echo sound.

Well hello, my little friend. I, too, understand the allure of one's own voice in an enclosed space. We have shower stalls and large empty rooms. It is easy enough, when in such a space, to take to singing or presenting a lecture with the illusion that one is alone and thus unheard. If I cannot see anyone, the logic goes, then no one can hear me. And so, such a chamber turns into a private theater of flamboyant declarations and soaring soliloquies while out-of-sight neighbors chuckle and grin at the unintended amplification.

Fences

I DIDN'T INTEND TO keep bees. But then again, I didn't intend to have a rabbit, poultry, or many of the other animals I've had over the years.

B began in his teens. He learned from an uncle who kept pallets of beehives in the mountain forest. The uncle learned his trade from an elder relative, the elder learned from someone even older, and so on. The origins of a family tradition often get lost in memory or unwritten history. We have just always done this; it's always been this way.

I took to assisting B with his bee work, as one does when one's partner has a complex or unusual hobby that one is entirely uninterested in. Hold the ladder, carry things, write notes on a clipboard.

One afternoon, while B was at work, one of his hives swarmed. The robust colony had grown to a healthy size, so the colony split itself, the queen and half the bees leaving to create a second colony somewhere else. If left to their own devices, the emigrating bees were vulnerable to dying from exposure, starvation, or being eaten by predators. They had to be caught and kept safely in a hive.

I had seen B deal with swarms, so I knew what to do. I assembled a hive from equipment in the garage, set up a tall ladder beneath the tree branch where the voyaging bees had gathered, put on a beekeeping veil and gloves, and set to relocating the bees into the hive.

Moving a swarm of bees is like trying to scoop soft, warm sand into a bowl ... in zero gravity. They slip and drip about, spilling like plush droplets that levitate and swirl around your head, a murmuration of furry insects. If the situation is ideal, and you know a few tricks, you may be able to pour them straight into the hive or to convince them to go in on their own. But often, the bees don't entirely behave the way you'd like them to.

This swarm appeared relatively cooperative. I carefully cut the thin tree branch they were on and laid it atop the open, empty hive, hoping the bees would be lured in by the scent of the honeycomb. At first, they did; the bees trickled off the branch and down into the hive. I pulled off one of my leather gloves and carefully, gently rested my outstretched hand beside the bees, then nudged the branch over it. Hundreds of tiny bees, quick and tickly, darted across my skin and down into the hive. Their hum vibrated like a cat's soft purr. And even in the heat of the afternoon, their warmth and soft, sweet scent rose like music.

When the branch and my hand were bare, all the bees now exploring the inside of their new hive, I discarded the branch, put the lid on the hive, and turned the hive so its entrance faced west, allowing the bees to use the sun to orient themselves. I took off my veil and other glove, looking forward to proudly telling B that I'd saved his bees.

Then I looked up.

DAVY KEEPS LETTING his cats outside. The day he moved into the Clydesons' rental house, we warned him. "There are coyotes here," we said. "Keep your cats inside."

"My cats stay close to me," he said. "They know better than to wander off."

"Keep your cats inside," we said.

WE HUMANS MARK our territories with our creations: signposts, fences, doors, the walls of buildings, arbitrary lines drawn on paper. We use materials from outside our selves: wood, rocks, limestone, metal. We create these objects to control our movements and those of others, to keep ourselves contained, separated, protected. We put up these barriers to contain us and our possessions, to keep us secure and separate from each other and from the wild. We build boxes to keep ourselves in and others out.

Animals mark their territories with their bodies: urine and claws, territorial pissings and scratchings and behaviors. The dog pees on a stone. The bird calls from a branch. The bear stands on its hind legs and rakes its claws down the trunk of a tree. Their scents and calls and markings are their fences, their signposts. "Here there be danger. Stay out." Or, "Here there be friends. Welcome; come in."

I LOOKED UP. On another branch of the same tree I had just removed the bees from was a clump of bees.

I lifted the lid of the hive: yes, there were bees in there, but fewer than before. And those that were left were moving toward the entrance, flying out, and rejoining their comrades in the tree.

A colony of bees is bonded to their queen by scent, pheromones. They will gather around her and shield her with their bodies, protect her with their lives. If separated from her, they will seek her out, follow her smell, and gather around her.

Apparently, the queen was not among the bees I'd relocated into the hive. She may have been jarred loose when I cut the branch, and while I was reveling in the tickling, tiny bees crawling over my hand, she was flying around my head or had landed on another branch in the tree. And her family, of course, had rejoined her.

Resolving to be gentler and more cautious this time, I again donned the beekeeping gear, climbed the ladder, and set to rehoming the bees.

As I lay the second severed branch on the hive, I knelt beside it and watched the bees closely, looking for the long abdomen of the queen to ensure she was there.

She wasn't. And again, the bees returned to the tree. Cursing mildly, I climbed the ladder a third time.

This time, I saw the queen among the bees and watched as she wiggled down into the hive. I had finally succeeded in catching B's swarm.

As I folded the ladder, I glanced up into the canopy of that poor tree, victim of my bee-guided, ad hoc pruning. Although there was a gaping hole in one side where three branches had been obviously removed, surprisingly, it didn't look terrible.

And beside that hole was a tidy cluster of honey bees.

Like perfume on an extravagant woman, the queen's pheromones do not always stay exactly where she is. They are pungent and persistent, sometimes lingering where she *was* instead of following her to where she *is*. A few vigorous puffs of smoke from a beekeeper's smoker tool in the area where the swarm landed will neutralize her scent, so any random bees flying about will flock to where she actually is.

But I knew nothing of this. I had no interest in keeping bees and knew only what tidbits of information I had gleaned from talking to B as he worked with his bees. I only knew that to be saved, the bees had to be put in a hive.

Sighing in frustration, I again ascended the ladder, cut a branch, and moved bees. There were far fewer this time, but I was determined to not abandon this clump of stragglers.

And again. And again. Each time, the cluster of bees returning to the tree was smaller.

By the time the number of bees returning to the tree was too few to bother—perhaps a few dozen, or a hundred—one side of the tree was nearly bare of branches. The tree looked like it had been attacked by a performance artist wood carver who had danced in front of the plant while waving about a machete.

Over dinner that evening, I told B about catching his bee swarm and explained why the tree now looked so disheveled.

He chewed his steak thoughtfully, swallowed. "You touched them last," he said. "Those are your bees now."

AT DUSK, I hear Davy calling his cats in, his voice harsh and beer thick. He sounds like an angry cow braying. This is how I learn his cats' names.

When I run into him at the community mailbox at the end of our street, he complains.

"The cats keep wandering off," he says. "They know they're supposed to come in at night. And the coyotes come around at night."

"Keep your cats in," I say. "Coyotes don't use clocks."

I DIDN'T INTEND to be a beekeeper, but suddenly I was. And I had so many questions about what to do next, how to take care of them. B answered what he could, but his knowledge was finite in comparison to my endless queries about the details of biology and life cycles. I turned to the internet, books, and beekeeping groups, and I read. I read and read. And every ten days, while B suited up to tend to his long row of honey bee colonies, I'd open my one small hive of bees to inspect it. I marveled at the queen's spiraling pattern of eggs and larvae, the glistening cells of new honey, the small mysteries and new questions that were created by each venture into the hive.

My hive thrived, grew; I split it into two hives, then three. At mealtime, I'd regale B with whatever new information I'd learned that day. My questions became fewer, my explanations longer. B gifted me half his hives. Instead of him telling me about what was going on with the bees, we'd discuss them mutually, colleagues working in tandem.

A few years later, I overheard him telling a new friend about the bees. He used to say, "I'm a beekeeper, and sometimes my wife helps me." This time, he said, "We're beekeepers."

A HONEY BEE colony is a superorganism, its bees functioning as individual cells within a complex, multi-organ body rather than as independent entities that are able to survive on their own. The queen is in charge of reproduction within the colony, as she is generally the only bee to lay eggs, and she is thus often likened to an ovary with wings. This is a misleading metaphor, for it implies that she has the capability of creating a separate being, much as a mammal gives birth to a baby. But she is more like bone marrow, creating blood cells that replenish the body and continually replace older cells as they die off.

The colony reproduces by splitting into two or more colonies, like an amoeba. The queen and half the bees depart the hive, creating a huge cloud of bees that may be up to two hundred feet in diameter and reach higher than a three-story building. The queen lands on a random object, and all the swarming bees gather around her in a protective clump. Scout bees search for a suitable place for the new colony to live and report back to the swarm. All the bees then fly to their new home.

Back in the parent colony, the bees left behind start creating one or more queens to replace the one that left. A queen bee is just a worker bee larva that has been fed exclusively royal jelly, a nutrient-rich goo that the bees make for feeding queens, instead of the usual baby bee diet of primarily pollen. The departing queen has left behind plenty of eggs and larvae for them to raise.

Honey bees are not native to most continents. They originated in Eurasia. On all other continents, any "wild" honey bees are just swarms from beekeepers' hives and the descendants of said swarms. They are feral colonies akin to packs of stray cats or dogs that result from people misplacing or abandoning their pets and allowing them to fend for themselves in the strange environment, breeding and spreading haphazardly, suffering from untreated injuries and disease. If caught and rehomed by a knowledgeable beekeeper, a honey bee swarm—like a lost cat or stray dog—can be kept safe and healthy. If ignored in the strange wilderness, they are likely to suffer unnecessarily and die miserably.

LATE AT NIGHT, I hear a rush of movement outside the window, a quiet meow.

The dark is never silent: snapping twigs, rustling branches, the soft thumps and snufflings of deer in the garden, the whistling shriek of a rabbit caught by an owl. It is pointless to look, to try to catch a glimpse: human bodies are loud and clumsy, and wild animals slip away like mist.

In the morning as I fill the bird feeders, a tuft of blond fur blows across my foot. It is too pale to be rabbit, too feathery and soft to be coyote. I walk in the direction it came from and find, dark against the green grass, a small cloth collar, frayed and broken, its dangling name tag smeared with clotting rusty brown.

Davy is on his porch, bellowing his cat's name.

BEES DO NOT share human knowledge and insight. People say that bees understand that the world is full of danger and the beekeeper is protecting them. People say that bees willingly relinquish their honey in exchange for such care and keeping. But bees have not been educated about the same scientific research or read the same books that the beekeeper has. They do not have insight into the chemistry of anti-parasite treatments, the thermoregulating properties of an insulating blanket wrapped around the hive in the winter, or what happens to their honey after it is removed from their hive. They do not understand human economics, the exchange and trade of goods and services, much less the subjective value we place on their honey.

As little as we currently know about the psychology of honey bees, we can at least say confidently that bees do not have a comprehensive understanding of the world beyond their experience. They don't have insight into what the beekeeper does or why or what could possibly happen to them if these things weren't done.

Using *if* requires an understanding of the idea of possibility, of potential outcomes. The thought *If we abandon this place, we may succumb to hardship, illness, tragedy, or death* requires that one has a concept of what these things are—which one can only have if one has experienced or been told of these things.

Humans communicate with each other, sharing stories, recommendations, and warnings. *Frank cut his foot while swimming in the river and got a terrible infection. If you take this pill, you'll sleep better at night. Don't eat the chicken at that restaurant—you'll be on the toilet for days.*

While honey bees do communicate with their hive mates, conveying important information and materials like neurons and blood cells do within a body, colonies do not communicate with other colonies. Thus, a colony that dies is a dead end: there can be no lesson learned, no warning gleaned from its demise.

It is unrealistic to assume that a colony of bees makes conscious decisions based on avoiding the possibility of hardship, suffering, or death. They are creatures of instinct: their behaviors have evolved to maximize their potential for survival. If the living conditions within a hive are so unbearable, so riddled with disease or parasites or structural damage that the survival of the colony is threatened, they will abandon the hive. But if the colony is not under threat, if the living conditions are reasonably suitable, the bees will not leave. If it is comfortable, safe, and suits their needs, why would they go elsewhere?

DAVY IS FURIOUS at the death of his cat. He demands to know what time the coyotes come out and why they don't just eat the rabbits and rats and leave the housecats alone.

"Keep your cat inside," I say. "Coyotes don't use clocks. And they eat whatever's in front of them."

HONEY BEES DO not stay in their hives out of loyalty to the beekeeper. Bees know what a face is, but they do not *know* an individual human. Perceiving a face as a face is not the same as the ability to recognize or distinguish individual faces, much less assign to them subjective characteristics like personality and intention.

A beekeeper's ability to open a hive of tens of thousands of bees without being stung may seem mystical or other-worldly, but it is no more unusual than the ability to pat a dog without getting bitten. To a person who has never spent time around dogs and has little knowledge of their behavior save for the fact that they bite, there is no discernible difference between a dog that is snarling with hunched back and bared teeth and one that is wagging her tail with perked ears. A person familiar with the body language of dogs, however, knows the difference and which dog is safe to pat. A knowledgeable beekeeper knows which factors—weather, hive health, food supply—affect the bees' moods and when to take extra precautions against getting stung. They pay attention to the language of the bees—the pitch of a hive hum, the scents of the pheromones, the patterns of their movements—to discern the bees' moods and adjust their behavior accordingly.

Most importantly, an experienced beekeeper is calm around their bees. They may have their worries, but they are not frantic.

All complex animals exude pheromones. When we experience an emotion, our bodies are flooded with complex chemicals and hormones. These substances essentially cause us to smell like our emotions. If a person near a beehive is anxious or afraid, the smell of fear acts like an alarm bell, alerting all bees in the vicinity and sending them into a panic. The bees have no way of knowing that the person is,

in fact, afraid of *them.* They know only that there is something to be afraid of and defend against. And so, they will
react defensively and aggressively, often stinging whatever
is in the immediate area that could possibly be the threat.
Someone who remains calm around bees will not spark such
a response.

The idea that a colony of bees will become familiar with
and thus accept their beekeeper is a far stretch. Worker
honey bees—which comprise 99 percent of a hive's population—only live for about six weeks. Only the first few
weeks are spent in the hive; thereafter, they graduate to
foragers, spending their days gathering pollen and nectar
and only returning to the hive briefly to drop off their wares.
A good beekeeper will open a hive once every ten days to
inspect it. Within a bee's entire lifetime, then, a beekeeper
will only visit the hive maybe a half-dozen times, at least
three of which will likely occur when that bee is away from
the hive. And given that a colony contains thirty-five thousand to sixty-five thousand bees, all of whom are constantly
moving about, busy with their tasks, what are the chances
that the same bee will interact with the beekeeper the two
or three times both beekeeper and bee are in the hive at the
same time?

We love bees, but they do not love us.

ANTHROPOMORPHISM: THE ACT of assigning humanlike
qualities or characteristics to non-human entities and inter-
preting their behaviors according to human emotions and
values. For example, when one assumes that an animal is
showing his teeth because he is smiling and thus expressing happiness. Or when we project our own desire or need
of a varied diet, clothing to cover our bodies, or frequent

physical contact with other beings onto animals in our care. These misinformed ideas are at best benign; at worst, they are harmful and dangerous to the animal that these beliefs are imposed upon.

By extension, anthropomorphism includes the mindset that animals will respect our human values and behave accordingly. Like humans that follow the rules, animals that stay contained within our boundaries and behave as we wish them to are perceived as cooperative and good. Animals that disregard our guidelines and behave in ways we are inconvenienced by are seen as uncooperative and bad, even malicious. The butterflies that look pretty and pollinate our gardens are good. The beetles and mice that invade and destroy our possessions are bad.

This mindset comes from the idea that all creatures exist in a hierarchy: humans above, animals below. Larger and more predatory animals are higher in the hierarchy, smaller and non-predatory animals are beneath them, and further down are even smaller creatures, insects, worms, and single-celled organisms like viruses and bacteria. The beings higher on the hierarchy are assumed to have control over or profound effect on those below them. Often, this authority is based on consumptive or predatory behaviors: The fox eats the mouse. The bear kills the fox. The human shoots the bear. A human can possess a fox, a mouse, and a bear and thus holds sway over their lives and well-being, but none of these animals can own a human. So, these animals must be somehow less than us, and we must therefore have authority over them.

This imposed hierarchy is rooted in religious dogma (a god creates and controls) or Western values of property (the subjective valuation of beings and objects that can be purchased, owned, sold). Nature, however, does not subscribe to human religious beliefs, and nor is it educated in economics. A microscopic virus will kill a human as easily as a bear or another human will. Animals do not look up to us for guidance or authority. They do not worship us. They do not understand our values, our rules. They do not respect our boundaries, boxes, and walls. They do not read our road signs.

***

DAVY'S OTHER CAT keeps coming over. He got her a kitten as a companion, but she's still looking for her missing friend.

"Keep your cats inside," I tell Davy. "Coyotes are opportunistic and go after anything smaller than them."

Davy is skeptical and does not know what *opportunistic* means. He waves his beer can like a weapon and threatens to kill the coyotes if he sees them.

***

BEE SWARMS TEND to land in random and often bizarre places. Sometimes, they alight on a low-hanging tree branch or fence post where they can be easily seen and easily retrieved. Sometimes, they fly into a forest, gathering high on a lofty tree, visible to the sharp eye but far out of reach. Occasionally, a swarm chooses a place to land that is inconvenient or awkward for other beings: a steering wheel, an armchair, the doorway of a doghouse or outhouse. In the spring and summer, beekeepers who are known to their neighbors and the public frequently receive frantic messages from strangers who have encountered swarm clumps or even established feral colonies on their property. *Please help*, the concerned message generally says. *There are so many bees, and I am worried for their safety.* Or, *I am worried for my safety.*

Ideally, a beekeeper responding to such calls for help would do so by donning their superhero beekeeping suit, gathering their tidy toolbox of swarm-catching equipment, and driving to the location in their small, round, yellow-and-brown-striped Volkswagen Beetle. They'd have a yellow flashing light on the car's roof with a pair of spinning wings on its sides, and the horn would make a loud buzz instead of a honk.

Instead, the beekeeper typically quickly gathers an assortment of equipment and tools—with any luck, remembering their smoker tool and baggy, protective canvas suit—into their family car or truck and sets off to the swarm location. They must move quickly: a landed swarm may leave at any moment, without notice. It is only when they arrive on the scene that the beekeeper can definitively pinpoint what exactly the situation is.

The public often uses the phrase "a swarm of bees" to refer to any group or gathering of small, buzzing insects. A hive of wasps is a swarm of bees. An established colony of honey bees is a swarm of bees. A few dozen bumblebees collecting nectar from a patch of clover, or a handful of native mason bees or carpenter bees burrowing into an old tree stump, is a swarm of bees. A hundred predatory hornets feasting on refuse in a garbage can is a swarm of bees. A cloud of houseflies is a swarm of bees. And sometimes, a swarm of bees is actually a swarm of bees.

An inexperienced beekeeper who responds to a swarm call will arrive, excited and hopeful, in anticipation of both being a stranger's hero and obtaining a free colony of bees. They are often disappointed to find that the creatures in question are not in fact honey bees but rather one of the other thirty thousand similar species of honey bee-like insects.

The caller, however, is still hopeful. They have a problem—a bunch of annoying or frightening bugs have gathered on their car's windshield or have nested in their house's rafters—and The Expert has come to the rescue.

This situation often results in a series of awkward questions:

Even though they're not honey bees, you'll still gather them up and take them away, won't you?

No, I'm a beekeeper, not a waspkeeper or a flykeeper.

But don't you want them for their honey?

Honey bees are called honey bees because they produce so much honey that we can harvest the excess. Other species do not, which is why they are not called honey bees.

Can't you just put them in one of your hives?

That would be as weird and inappropriate as trying to keep penguins in a chicken coop.

Won't they die if you don't save them?

Native bees don't need to be moved and put in special homes. And nobody's advocating for saving the wasps and hornets. Wild, native insects don't need to be removed from their natural habitats.

So, what do I do now?

If they're not causing a problem, leave them where they are. Leave native, wild creatures alone; they don't need your interference. And if they are causing a problem, call a pest-removal service, preferably one specializing in insects.

But you have to remove them—I'm a taxpaying citizen!

So? So am I. I'm not your on-call employee.

… Are you sure you don't want them?

I'm quite certain I don't.

I TRY TO resist petting Davy's cat or welcoming her when I see her on our property, but I can't bring myself to yell at her to go home when she is confused and grieving, missing her companion.

One afternoon, I find her sitting on our fence, silhouetted against the sunset. I stroke the soft fur of her ears and throat; she ducks her head down and presses her face into my hand, silently.

This is the last time I see her.

Davy stands on his porch, bellowing her name.

After a week, he stops.

***

WE PUT UP our fences—our walls, signposts, and boundaries—and are baffled, angered, or frustrated when animals don't behave accordingly. The deer leap over the fence. A dog finds an open gate and slips into, or out of, the yard. And as high as we build our fences and walls, as many signposts as we put up, the bees fly anyway, following their own maps drawn in song and smell and dance.

We reinforce our walls, put up stronger barricades, strengthen boundaries, close doors. But the animals pay no attention. Birds perch in the garage. Voles and snakes tunnel beneath concrete. Rabbits wander from one yard to the next, coyotes in pursuit. Wasps dangle their nests from eaves troughs and roofs. Even the homes we live in, the most personal and sacred spaces, are constantly invaded by small creatures that ignore closed doors and slip through cracks: ants, beetles, mice, flies, spiders.

Animals do not relate to human-made structures the same way we do. They do not understand our metal, wire, and wood creations, our walls of concrete and glass. They do not respect the squares and cubes we build: boxes, fences, houses. Our boundaries, to them, are arbitrary and meaningless.

This dismissive relationship is, in many ways, mutual.

B AND I catch a swarm, one of many this summer. We pour it into a box, then wait and hope.

A swarm, once caught and placed in a hive box, is not a viable colony of bees. It is a possibility.

Perhaps it has an illness, or a queen. Or not. Perhaps it absconded from its home due to an overwhelming infestation of parasites or disease, inadvertently bringing the ailment with them. Perhaps the queen was killed in transit, eaten in flight by a bird or hit by a car, and the hived swarm is but a box of random bees, aimless and nonviable without her royal pheromones and offspring to unite and replenish them. Perhaps it split from a healthy hive and has an enthusiastic young queen; perhaps in a few days, we will observe a spiral of tiny bee eggs in the comb, worker bees shooting like dark stars from the entrance, the warm hum and honey-rich scent of a thriving colony in its home.

Perhaps the colony's scouts will find a better home in the morning and abandon the one we have offered them in favor of one with more space, or less space, or a sweeter, less musty scent, or some other factor we are unaware of. Perhaps they will stay. There is no door or fence we can close against their possible departure, no signpost we can expect the bees to follow. We can only try to rescue them from the dangers we are aware of and present them with our handiwork, a house they can consider for their home, our clunky equipment and simple intentions crude offerings to these tiny gods.

Rude

A CAR PULLS INTO the driveway. I'm out working in the front yard, but we're not expecting any visitors, so I just smile and keep working. The driver stares at me. I stare back. I don't recognize him.

He looks down toward his lap. I assume he's texting the person he's trying to meet up with and will eventually figure out he's at the wrong address and leave. Nope.

He holds up a large envelope with a delivery company logo on it but doesn't step out of the car to hand it to me.

I approach the car. He rolls down the window a tiny crack, slips the envelope through it, and rolls up the window lightningspeed. I pick up the envelope, see my name and address on it, and give a thumbs-up to indicate accurate delivery.

He pulls out of the driveway so fast that his tires skid on the gravel.

That was rather antisocial, I think. *If he doesn't like encountering people, perhaps he should find work in a different industry.*

I adjust my beekeeping hat, wave away a few of the hundreds of bees that are buzzing around me, and turn back to the six-foot-tall beehive I am working on.

PART 2

Summer

WHILE WALKING THROUGH the woods, I found a stinging nettle plant—I'm not sure exactly when, but the welts on my legs tell me I did. And a snake, which I tried, unsuccessfully, to pick up. And some wild berries, which I ate but wasn't sure what they were.

I'm not sure how I manage to feign being an adult, because apparently, I'm about four years old.

Starfishes

I DIDN'T INTEND TO keep birds.

But then again, I didn't intend to keep bees either.

"WOULD YOU LIKE to be a robin momma?" asks the egg lady down the road. She has a yard full of assorted poultry and sells her chicken eggs from a fridge on her back porch. She knows I like critters, and this afternoon, she found on her lawn a small blue egg the size of her thumb joint. Perhaps it was stolen from a nest by a hungry predator and dropped. Perhaps its mother evicted it from its home due to infertility or deformity. Perhaps it is uncracked and was kept warm by the sun. Perhaps it might still be viable.

She offers to tuck it into her egg incubator and, if it hatches, to give me the baby bird to raise and release into the wild. I am skeptical about the viability of an abandoned egg and wary of the legalities of possessing a native, wild animal, but I take her up on her offer. If nothing else, this will be a cute experiment, a little adventure, a distraction from daily drudgeries.

The days before the projected hatching date tick by. We reach the hatching date. Nothing happens. Perhaps development was delayed by a night spent cold and exposed on the lawn. Perhaps the chick has died. We wait the next day, and the next.

On the fourth day, the egg lady messages me. "The egg has hatched," she says. "But it's not a robin. I don't know what it is."

Intrigued, I set up a rubber bin in our spare room to house this mystery hatchling: heat pad, food tray, a floor of soft cloth and newspaper, a watering trough with marbles to prevent a clumsy chick from drowning.

The hatchling is surprisingly tiny, small enough to fit inside my loosely clenched fist, and covered in a velvet-soft yellow fluff. They look like a cartoon cotton ball with a beak and toothpick legs. They chatter constantly with tiny, mouse-like peeps, and I don't know whether they are male or female. This species cannot be sexed until they reach maturity at about a month or two. Until then, they are as sexless as a stone.

Recalling the little egg that was in the incubator, I realize that a day ago, this creature was folded up inside of it. Of course they are small: minus their coat of fluff that dried and puffed up after hatching, this entire animal was tucked into that little egg.

I set the chick on the kitchen spice scale I use for weighing jars of honey. The chirping fluffball wobbles on their tiny, spindly legs, cocks their head up at me, and poops. Bird and poop together weigh a quarter of an ounce.

SPARROWLIKE BIRDS SUCH as robins hatch naked, blind, and vulnerable. They can't stand up; they flop about on their nest like fat, naked infants and need to be constantly fed worms and bugs by their parents until they grow feathers and are able to fly and eat on their own.

Chicken-like birds such as turkeys and pheasants, however, hatch covered in down and can stand and eat on their own within a few hours.

Based on this, I conclude that this chattery cotton ball is not a swallow, towhee, finch, or any of the many other common birds that live in the area. They are too yellow to be a corvid, too small to be a misplaced offspring of one of the egg lady's chickens. They likely won't be identifiable until a week or two passes and they grow recognizable feathers.

At first, I plan to keep the hatchling in the nursery bin and tend to them a few times per day. But their tiny size and softness are irresistible. And I quickly realize that though they chirp constantly when left alone, when picked up and held, they quieten down and sit calmly or sleep. I place the tiny bird in my shirt pocket or cleavage for several hours a day. Perhaps the warmth and gentle pressure comforts them. Perhaps they need the companionship.

I weigh the chick daily, out of curiosity and to ensure they do not falter in steady weight gain due to malady or malnutrition. At first, they gain only a barely measurable amount of weight per day, but within a week, they hit a growth spurt and quickly outgrow their napping spot in my cleavage. I take to wearing loose flannel shirts: the chick snoozes in my breast pocket or pokes their head up and watches like a little onboard supervisor as I noodle around the house and yard tending to minor chores.

For exercise and a change of scenery, I spread newspaper on the kitchen table and set the chick down on it. The noisy cotton ball darts around like a battery-operated pet toy, and I grab them to keep them from running off the table. A tiny bird has no concept of height or falling and no fear of edges.

When the bird grows tired or overwhelmed, their tiny peeps escalate into shrill cries. I rest my hand, cupped like a tent, on the newspaper, and the chick ducks under it, snuggles against my fingers, and quietens.

Tiny feathers begin to poke through and obscure the downy fluff. The aptly named pinfeathers appear like needles or porcupine spines. In the backyard dirt, I find a tiny doll's hairbrush with a head the size of my thumbnail; I wash the grime from its bristles and use it to gently groom the emerging feathers, breaking and pulling off their plastic-like coatings so the new feathers spring open like fans.

With their gangly, bare legs, rapidly growing torso, and mismatched, patchy feathers and fluff, the chick looks like a gawky preteen on the verge of puberty. I imagine them wearing too-short pants that end at the ankles and an outdated, parent-selected hairstyle, lisping through a mouthful of orthodontic work.

I send the egg lady photos. "I think that's a quail," she says and mentions the small pen of Coturnix quails she keeps in the corner of her chicken yard. We consider this and conclude that some clumsy predator, a crow or rat perhaps, stole an egg from her quail pen and accidentally dropped it on her lawn where she'd found it and rescued it.

I am relieved to learn this is not in fact a wild animal: I do not have to figure out how to rehabilitate them and release them back to nature, nor do I have to consider what will happen if releasing them fails, and I am left illegally possessing a native, wild bird. This is merely a misplaced farm animal. It belongs in a pen with others of its kind. And there is such a pen just down the road from me.

But the egg lady can't take the chick back right now. They are far too young to be added to her pen of adult quails: when encountering a smaller infiltrator, a flock may simply attack. I agree to foster the bird until they reach full growth.

Aware that naming something acknowledges its perceived personality and assigns it an identity that one can bond with and become attached to, I decide that this creature shall remain nameless. Instead, I refer to them as the birb, the intentional misspelling a nod to the chick's cartoonish cuteness. B avoids holding or interacting with the birb; he has a big, soft heart and does not want to fall in love, then have to say goodbye.

The birb is now too active and noisy to be left alone in their tub all day but too large to carry around in a pocket. I cut the top and bottom off a large, sturdy cardboard box to make a simple pen and place it on the lawn beside me while I work in the garden. The birb tears at the grass, chases little bugs, and dozes in the sunlight. I have no concerns about them escaping or flying off; they have little concept of the world beyond the cardboard walls, and until their adult wing feathers come in, they can only hop about.

In the evenings after dinner, the birb rests on my lap like a house cat while I type on my computer or sit on the porch, a handful of tissues close at hand in case of any random birb bathroom accidents. When they get restless and start chirping, I return them to their bin in the spare room to eat, drink, or poop.

And the bathroom accidents are frequent. Unlike cats and dogs, birds do not hold their bowels and empty them in specific locations. Quails will provide a little warning, often chirping, then standing up and taking a few steps backward before raising tail and letting loose, but otherwise, they excrete frequently, unapologetically. The fragrance is rich and unappealing. The birb's bin needs to be cleaned daily.

The house pets are intrigued by the scent and the noises of this strange little creature, but the spare room's closed door prevents them from investigating. Both the cat and the dog follow me about when I am carrying the birb: the dog thumping his tail against the wall joyfully, and the cat peeking cautiously from around corners.

I hold the birb at eye level to the cat: she sniffs curiously, then reaches out a paw to touch them. I snap my fingers and hiss a warning. She quickly learns that the birb is not to be touched and thereafter responds to their presence by turning her back dismissively and tucking her paws under her belly.

I show the birb to the dog: he sniffs them gently, then swipes his big, slobbery tongue across them in an enthusiastic kiss and sits back on his haunches. In the yard he chases rabbits, not birds, so I have no concerns about him being a threat to the birb's safety. The birb chirps in indignant protest, ruffling their feathers in response to the good-intentioned but unwelcome dampness.

Confident that the house pets will not cause problems—though I keep an eye on the cat lest she forget her manners—I let the birb walk about the kitchen floor while I wash dishes or put away groceries. They putter about like a tiny housemaid, eating fallen crumbs and occasionally commenting on the decor. When they are done wandering and ready for some downtime, they sit in a soft lump beside or on my foot until I pick them up and return them to their tub in the spare room.

I take the birb for outdoor walkies: first on the covered porch, then on the fenced lawn, always walking alongside them and keeping an eye on the sky for predatory hawks. My little feathered companion runs about like a joyous toddler, chasing bugs and peering closely at tree trunks and dandelions, happily chirping. When they have had enough of exploring, they stand on my foot until I scoop them up and tuck them into the crook of my elbow like a soft football.

I post photos of the birb's adventures on the internet. Friends comment that I'm a quail momma now. I protest, insisting that I am only fostering for a few weeks.

"You named it," the egg lady says and laughs. "That's your bird now!"

I look down at the nearly grown Birb contentedly snoozing in my lap and realize she's right.

FACED WITH THE realization that I now have a pet quail, I research the species and learn that they are flock animals. It would be cruel to keep one alone without companions and even crueler to keep it in a plastic bin indefinitely. And while a smelly bird in the spare room can be tolerated for a few weeks, neither B nor I want that situation to become permanent.

Legally, poultry can be kept in pens that are ridiculously small, several birds crammed into a few feet of space. I have seen people keeping quails in such pens: tiny, cramped spaces offering little comfort and no amusement. But these regulations are designed to accommodate the agricultural industry in which such animals are raised en masse for food production and are typically slaughtered early in life. They are designed to keep livestock secure and alive in as minimal accommodation as possible, with little regard for the creatures' happiness and well-being. They are not intended for the long-term housing of animals, kept until they die naturally.

After asking me a few questions, B disappears into his workshop. A muffled cacophony of industrious noises ensues: sawing, drilling, banging, colorful cursing.

He emerges many hours later and assembles on the lawn a huge wood-and-wire cage. Six by six feet, this poultry palace stands close to four feet tall and has a large hinged door I can walk through while stooped.

B returns to his workshop and exits carrying a miniature wooden doghouse with a peaked roof and fist-sized entrance. I am at first puzzled, but B then sets it inside the quail pen. It is a birdhouse, a cozy shelter for Birb to sleep in; the rest of the pen is their yard.

I retrieve Birb from their smelly indoor bin and place them in the new outdoor pen, then sit down on the lawn to watch.

Birb is accustomed to being outdoors, but the cage's wire walls are confusing: you can see through them, but you cannot go through them. After bumping into the walls a few times, Birb becomes distracted by a trail of delicious ants, attacks a wobbly thatch of tall grass, and discovers a small, bare patch of dry dirt. They flop on their side, scratching feet and flapping wings, creating a cloud of dust that covers them—their first dust bath.

After an hour, I return Birb to their indoor bin. An afternoon in the outdoor pen is delightful I'm sure, but a sudden night outdoors would be shockingly cold and lonely. I decide to gradually acclimatize Birb to their new home before moving them outdoors permanently.

For the next few days, I put Birb in the outdoor pen with a water trough and food tray and leave them there until the air cools in the evening. I check on them frequently, like a parent peeking into a child's room to watch them at play.

I spend the afternoons working in my garden or with the beehives, a few dozen feet from Birb's cage. Their contented chirping—now more a high-pitched burbling than a chick's sharp peeps—blends pleasantly with the symphony of the songbirds. When it rises to a shrill scream, I at first come running, fearing some injury, only to realize Birb has suddenly noticed they're alone and wants to know where I am.

After a while, I respond to such panicked calls by calling out from where I am; Birb's alarm subsides quickly and returns to a mellow, pleasant chatter.

When Birb sees me, they bow like a tiny, fat butler, then hop forward two or three times. I learn that this is a quail's way of expressing joy, and I am delighted when I am greeted with such enthusiasm. Sometimes, Birb runs away from me and hides behind their little birdhouse, then peeks around the corner—and when we make eye contact, they jump back into hiding with a sharp chirp, then peek around the other side of the house.

B hears me laughing, watches the silliness, and asks, "Are you playing peekaboo with a bird?"

Yes. Yes, I am playing a baby's game with a farm bird. I tap my hands on the pen's frame and call, and Birb comes running toward me. It occurs to me that Birb was raised by a human being, with only a slobbery dog as an occasional companion. Birb likely thinks they are a dog or a very small human. Birb definitely needs birb friends.

BIRB SPENDS THEIR last night indoors. I get a pair of day-old Coturnix quails from a local breeder, relocate Birb to the outdoor pen, and put the chicks in the bin in the spare room. They are tiny, and Birb is nearly full-grown; it will be several weeks before the little ones have grown enough for all three birds to be kept together without the possibility of fights and injuries. And the bin is now far too small for Birb to live in comfortably. It is the same size as the battery cages commercial quail farmers keep multiple quails in, and Birb needs room to run around.

The chicks are very affordable, and the new outdoor pen could fit many more, but I only get two. I have heard many stories of chicken math, the phenomenon in which someone buying a few units of live poultry ultimately ends up with several dozen or hundreds, and I only need a few quails to keep Birb company. I don't want to keep poultry. But now I have three birds.

At first, I follow the same methodology with the chicks that I did with little Birb: I tuck them inside my shirt or pocket for warmth and comfort, carry them around like babies. I quickly realize, however, that they have each other and don't need me for companionship. I occasionally hear one of them shriek out a lonely cry, but when I look in on them, I find they are merely facing away from each other and are thus unaware of each other's presence. Object permanence is not a baby quail's strongest cognitive skill.

In the morning after Birb's first night alone, I rush outside, hoping my little buddy has not been too traumatized. They do their happy hops, then run in large circles. When I tap my fingers on the open cage door to call them over to me, they instead hide behind their house to play peekaboo.

The chicks are fine and don't need much attention aside from food, water, and a daily housecleaning. Their bin is twice as fragrant and messy as when it was inhabited by Birb. In homage to the upcoming weeks of smelly birds in the house, I name one of the chicks Stinker.

Some of my friends say that the only reason to keep poultry is for eggs and meat, but I am not interested in eating my pets. In cheeky defiance, I name the other chick after the part of a meal that looks like food but is typically not eaten: Garnish.

I sit on the lawn and talk to Birb for a while before donning my beekeeping suit for a workday in the hives. Birb chirps and burbles cheerily, attacking bugs and scratching in their earthy dust bath, then retreats to their favorite spot to sit and watch the world: in the doorway of the little house, their little head poking out, bright eyes watching, looking altogether like a tiny, feathered guard dog.

ON THE EVENING of Birb's first full day in the outdoor pen, I step out onto the porch to take out the garbage. I hear a sudden flutter of wings and a squawk from Birb.

"It's okay, little buddy," I call toward the pen. "I'll see you in the morning."

I briefly consider sitting next to the pen and talking to Birb in the dark but change my mind and go back inside. Late-night conversations with an adorable little animal are appealing, but the demands of deadlines and to-do lists call louder.

The following morning, I stare out the window at the quail pen while washing dishes. I notice that Birb's water bottle is lying on its side. Their enthusiastic antics must've knocked it over. I'll have to refill it and figure out some way to keep it upright and stable.

I crouch down in front of the pen, pop the door open, tap my fingers on the doorframe, and call. But there is no answering burble chirp, no welcoming rush through the grass toward me. I retrieve the fallen water bottle and the food dish, which is also upturned and scattered. There is no sign of Birb.

Alarmed, I step inside the pen and pick up the little doghouse, expecting to find Birb—terrified, injured, or dead—inside it. But there is no Birb. I turn a slow, crouched circle inside the pen, looking for my little chirping friend among the grass and dirt. But I see only a few tiny golden feathers, scattered.

Confused, I step out of the pen and check the door latch. It closes firmly and shows no signs of having been tampered with—and it was closed when I arrived. I walk a circle around the outside of the pen, looking carefully for any damage or holes where a predator may have gotten in or a quail out. Nothing. On my second circle, I keep my eyes focused on the bottom edge of the pen where it rests on the ground. And then I see it.

In the far back corner, out of sight of the porch and hidden by a tuft of grass, is a small pile of fresh dirt. I crouch down and look closer. The dirt is on the edge of a hole the size of a clenched fist.

My ears whistle shrilly; my heart thuds. I jam my fingers under the edge of the quail pen and lift, tilting it above my head. I look down: the hole is a short tunnel that ends in a shadowed corner, behind a clump of grass, inside the cage. I look up: the underside of the pen's frame right above the tunnel is smeared with a dark reddish brown. A lone yellow feather is stuck to the drying blood.

I drop the cage and stand, turning in slow circles as I raise my dirt-covered fingers to my face. What did I do. What can I do. What, if anything, should I do. Could Birb still be alive, perhaps injured, perhaps viable. Is there still time. Should I look for them. There are no tracks in the grass, no trails left by a tiny hurt bird. Could I find Birb. What could I do. What should I do.

B sees me turning slowly on the lawn, the quail pen door open and swinging in the breeze, water bottle and food tray scattered uselessly. He hurries to me, his face thunderously dark and worried.

I point at the tunnel under the pen. "Birb's gone," I gasp. "There's only blood and feathers."

B wraps his big arms around me, glaring at the tunnel and the pile of blood-smeared dirt. "Mink," he growls.

And Birb's late-night flutter and squawk snaps suddenly into horrific context.

DECADES AGO, THERE were several mink farms in the area. Bred for their fur for the fashion industry, the mink lived in large locked cages that housed hundreds. A group of well-intentioned but misguided animal welfare advocates took to sabotaging the farms at night by opening the cages and setting the mink free.

After years of such protest and subterfuge, the mink farmers closed business and moved on. But the freed mink remained, breeding in the forests and feasting upon birds and small animals. The area was agricultural, populated by farmers and animal-loving hobbyists. Mink are vicious predators and will slaughter an entire coop of chickens within minutes, dragging a few select birds home to feed their offspring and leaving the rest as pointless thrill kills. The minks thrived—for a while.

***

I SIT ON the porch, dazed and numb, holding Stinker and Garnish for comfort. B flips the quail pen upside down to wash off the blood stain and staple a floor of heavy wire mesh to the bottom of the pen.

I did not want this. I did not want to have a birb. I did not want these two tiny chicks. And now my little buddy, my Birb who thought he was a dog, is dead. And these two peeping chicks are so small and so soft and so vulnerable. I did not want this, this sorrow, this hurt, this handful of tiny life. But now I am holding this.

This is a tunnel dug by a hungry mink into an extravagant pen that housed one dorky pet quail. This is the dissatisfaction of a small, corpseless death, no clanging shovels for digging graves or axes for vengeance, just a rattling silence and a cold hose to wash away evidence of a life. This is nature: surprising, uncontrollable, cruel. This is the crossing out of little joys. This is displaced rage: at a long list of dull to-dos and deadlines that rely too much on others while tiny creatures rely entirely on me for their well-being and survival; at wild animals behaving normally; at people; at a hungry mink. This is default guilt, regret. This is an empty water glass at the wrong time. This is a sighing recitation of all the obvious platitudes: *it'll be okay, life goes on, perspective, this too shall pass.* This is a poof of tiny, soft feathers across the lawn in the wind, cold water through holes in muddy yard shoes. This is a quiet resignation to all the truths.

THE QUAIL CAGE, now secured with a wire bottom that the grass pokes through but that prevents rodents from tunneling into, sits empty on the lawn, waiting until Stinker and Garnish are feathered enough to take up residence.

But our anger is not so stoic. We are furious, determined to take vengeance on the mink, and we daydream many violent and impractical ways to kill it.

Regardless of our thirst for revenge, the mink must be eradicated before it goes after my other little quails. But we hesitate to set out poisoned bait or deadly snap traps. I think of the summer week when I kept finding dead rabbits in our yard. They were oddly uninjured and exposed, stretched on the lawn as though dozing—a mystery, until we queried our then-neighbor about whether she was aware of any poisonous substance in the area. She brightly revealed she'd recently set out poison to combat the rats under her porch and was puzzled at our sighing, exasperated replies. "But it's rat poison, not rabbit poison," she'd said, confused.

Wild animals are opportunistic and do not understand when something is not intended for them. Poisons are especially problematic, as their effect is often delayed, resulting in chemical-laced small animals being caught and eaten by larger animals such as hawks, eagles, coyotes, wolves, and even domestic animals such as cats and dogs who are then themselves poisoned. Snap traps must also be carefully reconsidered, as they may inadvertently injure or kill welcome or beloved animals: rabbits, a neighbor's wandering house cat, the cheeky squirrels that take peanuts from our hands.

B retrieves from the garage a live trap—a cage-like device with a spring-loaded door designed to catch and contain rather than injure and kill. We set it up outside the quail pen and bait it with a spoonful of raw meat.

We don't exactly know what we'll do with the mink when we catch it. The ideas in our vicious, angry daydreams are tempting but unrealistic and unnecessarily cruel. Like anyone who has owned livestock and dealt with the pests that frequent agricultural properties, we know a handful of methods for killing small animals quickly and humanely without excessive mess. We can figure out which method to use on our furry archenemy later, after we've caught it.

Late at night, I hear a distinctive metallic snap in the yard. I shine a flashlight at the live trap. The trap's door is closed, and the wire cage is shaking as though something was thrashing about inside it. Trembling with nervous excitement, I tiptoe—unnecessarily—to the trap. I have never seen a live mink in person before. Will I think it cute or ugly? After it has been euthanized, will I have the stomach to skin it and learn how to tan a small hide so I can sew a luxuriously soft collar onto one of my coats? Or will I just feel twisted and sad and throw the dead mink into the forest while crying and cursing the waste of one death followed by another?

I squat next to the trap. Its occupant is now still. I can see no recognizable face, nor rodent-like profile or limbs, just a mass of dark fur. Intending to carry the trap to the porch so we can deal with our prisoner in the morning, I grab the trap by its handle and lift.

The mass of fur shifts and turns to reveal the flattened ears and needle-filled, snarling mouth of a house cat, hissing with such fury that I nearly expect it to spit sparks.

Setting the trap back down, I steady it with a foot and unlatch the door. The terrified cat bolts out and away.

The live trap catches nothing else for several months.

INSIDE THE HOUSE, the tiny quail chicks eat and poop and peep and grow, their wide, naive eyes unaware of the fatal danger outside and the work we are doing to protect them from it. In the afternoons, I put them in the cardboard-box pen beside me as I garden, and in the evenings, they snooze on my lap as I sit and type, but I am not as fastidious about handling and interacting with them as I was with their predecessor. They have each other.

I did not intend to keep poultry, but now I have these two tiny birds that were only obtained as companions for another bird that I no longer have. And after learning about the typical standards for quail housing, I do not feel comfortable gifting or selling these two to live in tiny cages. And B put so much work into designing and building the quail cage that now sits empty on our lawn. I believe quails only live for two or three years. I'm okay with taking care of a pair of quails for a few years.

Realistically, though, I might not end up with only a pair of birds. Two hens will be fine together, but roosters are aggressive. Each rooster needs at least three hens to avoid any one hen being overly mauled by his persistent, passionate advances. And two roosters may just fight. Mathematically, I only have a 25 percent chance of both chicks being female; ergo, I will likely have to get more hens to even out the ratio and ensure everyone is safe and happy. But I did not want to keep birds, much less more than two or three birds, so I hope and wait until the chicks are old enough to be sexed.

When Stinker and Garnish are a month old, fully feathered, and thus able to stay warm on their own, I move them permanently into the outdoor quail pen. My throat aches at the memory of Birb, but I calm my anxieties by double-checking that the wire bottom of the pen is secure and able to prevent any predatory rodent from tunneling in. I clean out the large plastic tub the chicks have been living in and am grateful for the opportunity to finally air out the spare room after nearly two months of living with the thick stench of poultry excrement.

Inspired by the birds' tendency to stay close to the edges of their pen and my explanation that wild quails prefer the shelter of shrubs and underbrush to open spaces, B disappears into his workshop and returns a few hours later with a wheelbarrow filled with an assortment of quail cage furnishings. A tray and bag of fine sand for a dust bath. A wide-mouthed PVC pipe cut into tunnel-like sections. Short, table-like platforms that the birds can walk over or hide beneath. Pieces of plywood to lean against other objects and create hiding spots.

For the first few nights in their new home, the quails remain undisturbed by any predator. On the fourth day, however, I see a row of holes and small dirt piles along the exterior of one edge of the quail pen. My stomach falls down an elevator shaft. I climb inside the pen, searching frantically for my birds. Stinker and Garnish are still there. I press my hands against the floor of the pen, pulling and pushing it, searching for any hole—but the wire mesh has done its job, and no creature has found its way into the pen.

Filling the holes and tamping the dirt piles down with my foot, I move the live trap to that side of the pen and again bait it with a small dish of raw meat.

Every morning for the next week, the beginnings of new holes appear around the edges of the quail pen. Each tunnel is only a few inches long and stops when it hits the protective wire flooring of the cage. And the live trap remains empty.

Baffled, we query neighbors for ideas of how to catch this elusive mink. They remind us that no mink have been seen or reported in our neighborhood for over a decade. What we do have, however, are rats. In this agricultural area, rats remain an ever-present pest that thrives on the spillage and garbage of feed and produce. And a rat will kill a small bird as easily and as hungrily as a mink will.

The oddly small mink holes suddenly make sense. We have not a mink but a rat—or, more likely, multiple rats. I lie down beside the quail pen, trying to see the world from a rodent's-eye view. I creep about on my belly with my cheek to the ground, peering through the overgrown lawn grass, until I see it: a subtle trail of parted grass, a rat-sized walking path, from the narrow space beneath our porch to the quail pen.

Rats are social animals: they live in colonies of dozens to hundreds, in tunnels and nests beneath the shelter and warmth of buildings and sidewalks. A single, easily avoided live trap will not eradicate such a colony. But then again, if the quails are safe and the rats pose no threat, perhaps we can just let the rats be.

IN THEIR GIANT cage, Stinker and Garnish require surprisingly little regular care. I refill their water and food daily and pick them up to check for injuries and ailments, but otherwise they pose virtually no demand. Their pen is so big and aerated, and they are so small, that it doesn't even need to be periodically cleaned. Their excrement just falls through the wire-mesh floor and crumbles into the soil.

The birds spend their days pecking at bugs, staring out the pen walls at the world beyond, and dozing like tiny puppies in the sunbeams. They seem to play rudimentary games: running in and out of the PVC pipe tunnels or hopping on and off pieces of wood. They lead simple lives but appear to be happy, or at least content.

ON MILD AFTERNOONS and in the cooling dusk after dinner, B and I often sit on the porch and watch the songbirds that flit to and from our bird feeders. A tiny Douglas squirrel has learned that if she approaches, she will be offered a handful of peanuts or sunflower seeds in a small bowl. If we fail to provide her with an offering, she skitters about the porch and pointedly stares at us or stands on her hind legs with her front paws folded politely at her chest.

One afternoon, our squirrel friend is oddly absent. There is only the usual menagerie of finches, grosbeaks, and nuthatches flitting about our bird feeders and gathering fallen seeds from the ground below.

A small whiskered nose pokes out from beneath the edge of the porch. It is too long, too brown, to be the squirrel.

A chickadee lands beneath the feeders, pecking at fallen seeds, its bold, black-and-white plumage sharp against the green and brown of the lawn. Focused on its crunchy meal, it turns its back to the porch.

The rat darts out from under the porch and across the lawn, heading straight for the unaware chickadee. I yelp in surprise and the bird flies off. The rat slows and, defeated, retreats under the porch.

Humans create delicious garbage and often keep animals that produce more delicious garbage or are themselves delicious. So, though the presence of rats is unwelcome, it is not unexpected. And unless one is living in a region that has eradicated rats through aggressive strategic methods, they can only be tolerated, their presence and its effects minimized.

But a rat attacking the local songbirds is not something we are willing to accept. And we are still angry about Birb's bloody death. We resolve, again, to go after the rats hard: to kill, to destroy, to wreak vengeance.

We set up rat snap traps along the rats' frequently traversed trails: by the compost bin, around the quail cage, next to the porch. The traps are hefty, brutal, jaw-like clamps that crush flesh and bone when they snap shut. We leash them to fence posts with heavy wire to prevent them from being dragged off in the case of a non-fatal snap and prop plastic bins overtop them to keep rabbits and birds out. Hoping to avoid inadvertently hurting the squirrel, we bait the traps with cat food and bits of raw meat, morsels that are appealing to predatory vermin but unattractive to creatures that eat seeds and nuts.

I relocate the live trap to beside the porch, where we saw the bird-hunting rat emerge. Perhaps it will again lunge toward a songbird and run blindly into the trap.

AT FIVE WEEKS of age, Stinker and Garnish are now full grown. Their chick peeps have deepened into duck-like honks, though occasionally they still lose sight of each other in the pen and let out a shrill, plaintive shriek of perceived isolation.

When I step inside the pen to change their water and top up their feed, or to add fresh sand to their sand bath, they burble at me quietly and peck at my shoes. Their beaks are short and dull, and they are too small to inflict any noticeable pain or damage, but they attack any small item that resembles a bug or worm. They are particularly interested in shoelaces.

One afternoon as I attend to their feeding, Garnish stands by my foot, stretches up to a full height of at least eight inches, peers up at me with a bright, beady eye, and lets out a throaty, rattling cry that sounds like an indignantly yelled *whatthefuck*.

I am startled, then laugh. My little Garnish has just crowed. Only roosters crow. I pick him up and examine his bum area, comparing it to photos I have seen on the internet, then do the same to Stinker. At the end of a month of waiting and hoping, I learn that my quails are both roosters. I have to get them some hens.

I do not wish to again repeat the process of raising smelly chicks in the house, and I want to add the hens as soon as possible lest the roosters take to fighting each other, so I opt for buying a dozen young hens from a local breeder.

Adding birds to an existing flock of poultry can be tricky. The established flock sees the new birds as infiltrators and may attack them. But if both new and old birds are put into a space that is unfamiliar to all of them, then the social hierarchy is disrupted, everyone feels equally disoriented, and no territorial fighting ensues.

Temporarily storing my little roosters in a lidded storage bin on the porch, I enlist B to help me drag the quail pen to a fresh spot on the lawn, then rearrange all the pen furnishings: tubes, boards, food and water troughs, the little house, sand bath, all are reorganized to form a new quail playground. Then I add the new hens.

At first, the hens are stunned and silent. They stand huddled together in the center of the cage, still as stones and terrified. To date, they have spent their entire lives in a barn in tiny cages or in bare, minimalistic brooder pens among dozens or hundreds of their chick cousins. In this new space, only the smell of the grainy food and the presence of the other hens are familiar. Everything else—the grass beneath their feet, the tubes and boards, the sunlight and shadow, the fresh air and sounds of outdoors—is strange and unknown.

I leave the hens to acclimatize and settle in. In the bin on the porch, Stinker and Garnish burble discontentedly and crow. *Whatthefuck. Whatthefuuuuck.*

In the meantime, I do my daily check of the rat traps, replenishing bait and disposing of the dead as needed. A dead rat left unattended does not concern me. It is the possibility of injured rats, animals with legs or tails broken and caught in the traps, unable to escape, that keeps me vigilant. Such creatures must be euthanized, not left to be tortured. I do not want the rats to live, but neither do I want them to suffer.

After an hour, the hens have overcome their initial shock and begin exploring their new home, pecking at the grass and flopping about in their dust bath like excited children at an amusement waterpark. I retrieve my roosters and add them to the pen. For a moment, they stand very tall and still, their necks long and eyes wide, then they begin to explore their surroundings and meet their new companions.

The next morning, I step into the quail cage to check on the birds and see if there has been any conflict or fighting. The hens, unaccustomed to the presence of a giant twolegs, rush to the back of the pen and hide, crouching low, attempting to disguise themselves as soft rocks or feathery clumps of earth. The two roosters step forward and stand at my feet, proud sentries protecting their frightened ladies. Garnish cocks his head and glares up at me threateningly. Stinker stretches up to his full height and barks a stern warning up at my left knee: *Whatthefuck.*

I scoop up the roosters and cuddle them like overgrown hamsters. They honk indignantly at me. I check them for injuries and blood spatters and, finding none, set them down. Stinker pecks benignly at my shoe, and Garnish sputters a half crow, then they appear to change their minds and return to pecking at the ground as the nervous hens come out of hiding.

None of the birds have any injuries. None of them are limping, spattered with blood from a frenzied attack, or cowering terrified in a corner. I will keep an eye out for any future bullying, for any birds that harass or attack the others or are isolated or attacked by their flockmates, but otherwise, the addition of the hens seems successful.

A few days later, I find, lying in the middle of the quail pen like forgotten luggage or a discarded piece of garbage, a tiny, beige-and-black-speckled egg.

"Who put this here?" I ask the hens. But they just stare at me.

Unlike chickens and wild birds, Coturnix quails do not typically incubate their eggs. They have been so overbred by the agricultural and pet industries that they have lost the instinct to protect their eggs and keep them warm. Instead of building nests, they just plop their eggs out like random poops wherever they are standing. They show no interest in their eggs and just leave them where they are laid.

Over the next few weeks, more eggs appear, scattered randomly about the pen. Some are speckled, others solid white or brown, and a few are a dreamlike baby blue. The hens settle into a laying schedule of one egg per hen per day. In cooking, five quail eggs equals one standard chicken egg. I save the eggs in the fridge, then scramble them into rich omelets or pickle them into jars of tiny preserves.

I did not want to keep birds. Now, I have fourteen and a constant supply of ridiculously tiny eggs.

THE LIVE TRAP that we set out for the rats and baited with assorted seeds and bits of meat catches various birds, who flutter and squawk resentfully until released, and one cottontail rabbit who refuses to exit when I open the trap door. Crouching very still, as though to make himself invisible, the bun doesn't even twitch a paw when I lift the trap to try to pour him out. I have to poke my fingers through the cage wires and aggressively shove at his haunches to get him to move. His fur is luxuriously soft. I wipe my fingers on the grass and inspect my hand for any fleas I may have inadvertently obtained.

The little red squirrel becomes a frequent occupant of the live trap. The first few times she is caught, she thrashes about inside the cage, banging into the walls and shrieking curses. The third time, however, she is calm. She stands on her hind legs and chirp-grunts in my direction, then leans one paw against the trap wall like an impatient little lady tapping her fingernails. I want to name her Stu, short for stupid, because she appears to not be learning to avoid the trap, but as a friend points out, "She gets an easy meal, and you always let her out, right?"

The live trap, however, catches no rats. I sometimes find rats dead and stiffening in the snap traps, but the live trap remains ratless. At first.

UNAWARE THAT THEY could have otherwise been living in tiny battery cages or slaughtered for meat, the hens settle into their oversized pen, scattering eggs at random as they enjoy a relatively luxurious lifestyle that is overseen by a duo of vigilant roosters. They seem to particularly enjoy using the PVC pipe tunnels B donated to their pen: a handful or more of them spend several minutes to an hour at a time running through a tube, popping out the end of it, turning around, and running back through it, back and forth, happily chirping. When I open the cage to replenish their food and water, the quails crowd around me like tiny, enthusiastic children, excited for the bowlful of dried mealworms or sliced zucchini I toss down for their dessert.

Once per month, I gather the birds into plastic bins on the porch, and we hose down the poop-covered pen furnishings and drag the pen to a fresh spot on the lawn. Our yard becomes a checkerboard of our regular lawn and lush grass and weeds where the soil has been fertilized with quail poop and seeded with leftovers from the birds' meals.

As winter approaches, we install a heat lamp in the quail pen and staple thick plastic sheeting over the wire-mesh walls to keep the birds warm and dry. The outside ground is now too wet, muddy, and snowy to move the cage onto, so instead of moving the cage to clean it, I muck it out like a barn: scraping and scooping up poop and refuse with a hand trowel, gagging and sneezing, while the birds crowd around me in anticipation of fresh sand in their dust bath and a scattered handful of tasty treats.

Wary of the wild rabbits, squirrels, and birds becoming more desperate in their winter search for food, we remove all the rat traps from the yard and box them up until spring.

The short, gray days of winter slip by like runny, cold mud.

AS THE WEATHER warms into spring and the relentless precipitation lessens, the quails molt, shedding their old feathers and growing new ones.

Poultry don't lay eggs when they're molting. This happens twice a year: the pen fills with loose, snowy feathers, and the birds huddle down, miserable, naked, and cranky as the spikes of new feathers poke through their skin. No eggs, for weeks or months. The quails eventually re-feather and return to their usual frisky selves, but still: no eggs. Perhaps it is still too cold, and the coop not insulated enough, for them to squat and squeal as they pop out their tiny eggs.

Then one day, there will be a lone egg, unclaimed and cooling in the dust bath. Perhaps there will be more. Many. Or only a few, random and unpredictable. Perhaps the hens have grown old and will lay less often now. Perhaps this egg will be the last one.

This is a poem. Or perhaps a metaphor. A prediction, perhaps, that won't be decipherable until time passes and the weather continues to warm, until the loss of discomfort and the regrowth of the new. Until then, we cuddle down, alone and naked and miserable, or wrap ourselves in whatever warmth we can grow. This is a metaphor, perhaps, of my life. Or of yours. Or of simply today.

ONE LATE SPRING morning, the quails seem oddly subdued. I creep inside the pen and survey my surroundings, at first noticing little that seems different. Two of the quails are sleeping, flopped on their side with their legs splayed out as they often do, looking rather deceased. Usually, they wake and hop upright when I approach the cage. But these two do not. And one of the birds' water bottles has been knocked over.

I nudge the two snoozing hens with a finger. They are cold, stiff. I see a pair of tiny feet poking out of a tube—another dead bird.

Frantically, I look in every hiding spot, behind every leaning board, inside the tiny houses, brushing aside curious quails with an arm. Altogether, I find four dead birds: three hens and Garnish, the smaller rooster. And one small brown hen, flopped on her side and smeared in blood, is still breathing but unable to stand. I inspect each of the surviving birds. They are frightened but appear uninjured. Even Stinker is quieter, less aggressive, but otherwise fine.

Alarmed and confused, I carefully inspect the cage from the inside. Did some creature get in and attack my birds? But nothing looks different except the random spatters of blood. Perhaps one of my birds got injured somehow and the others attacked it, the resulting mess provoking them into a frenzy of birds attacking each other? I have heard of such things happening to poultry farmers—but despite occasional minor injuries, I've never seen this phenomenon in my flock.

Finding no clues as to what happened, I open the pen door and toss the dead birds outside. One catches on a wire sticking out at the bottom of the pen door—I bend down to retrieve the bird, and then I see it.

Two of the heavy-duty staples attaching the wire mesh to the wooden frame of the door are popped loose, as though the wire had been forcefully pressed against from outside. The resulting gap in the wire is bent inward, curved to fit a small, sleek body the diameter of my fist, framed in sharp, loose wire ends.

The rats. A rat—or perhaps several of them—has broken into the pen and slaughtered my quails. None of my birds are missing; none were dragged from the cage or consumed. All the rats achieved was killing a handful of birds and injuring one horribly. Perhaps they killed for fun like their distant cousins the mink.

But the slaughter was incomplete. There are still uninjured birds, likely saved by my surviving rooster. I pick up Stinker and cuddle him. "Good boy," I whisper into his neck feathers. "You've done such a good job." He honks loudly and demands to be set down.

I did not intend to keep birds. Now, I have ten and a sorrowful mess to clean up.

CAREFULLY CRADLING THE injured hen in my hands, I ask B his opinion. Should this hurt bird be euthanized, or is she reasonably viable? The back half of her torso is a shredded mess of blood, poop, and feathers, and there is something soft and bloody sticking out of her bum. She can move her head and wings, and her neck is uninjured, but she cannot stand. Her eyes are bright and focused, and she has a surprising amount of energy. She is probably in a lot of pain, B agrees, and might have internal injuries. He also grew up surrounded by animals, both domestic and wild, and has seen creatures recover from a wealth of injuries. We are reluctant to euthanize a pet that may survive and have a reasonable quality of life.

We decide to isolate the bird indoors and decide in the morning.

Uncertain of her exact injuries and unwilling to leave her in such a shoddy state overnight, I give the hen a slow, careful bath with warm water and a soft cloth. The caked-on grime slips off, revealing a mess of broken feathers and gashed-open skin. Her left hip is particularly gruesome, the flesh torn open to the meat, as though a rat had bit and torn at her hip and thigh. The object protruding from her bottom, which I'd at first taken to be a prolapsed uterus or lump of internal flesh, turns out to be a partially formed egg, shell-less and squishy, lodged in her egg canal. I poke at its membrane; the soft egg tears open, draining yolk and albumen, then slides out easily.

After she is clean, I wrap her in a soft rag to dry and dab antiseptic cream on her wounds and bum. A plastic storage bin furnished with rags, a waterer, and a handful of dried mealworms makes a hospital room for her, and a tiny bit of painkiller dissolved in her drinking water serves as an ad hoc anesthetic. I will check on her later, tonight, and in the morning. She will either improve or worsen and need euthanizing. She will either live or die.

RETURNING TO THE quail pen to tidy it up and bury the dead, I find B with a staple gun, assorted pieces of wood, a nail gun, and a handful of zip ties. He has fixed the rat hole in the pen door and is now strategically circling the pen, doubling the number of staples securing the wire mesh to the pen's frame and reinforcing the areas the rats appear to have been gnawing at. He punctuates his work with a steady stream of Latverian curses. The quails cower in a corner and stare at him silently.

"I don't like birds," he grumbles. "But these birds are pets. And pets are family. And I will go after anyone, or anything, that hurts a member of my family."

He unearths our collection of rat traps from the garage; I retrieve a shovel and bucket and set to burying my poor dead quails.

My throat feels like stone; my stomach is hollow and aching. B stomps about, cursing and slamming doors. This is the second time the rats have attacked and killed our poultry.

Our eyes are narrowed and focused, sharp and clear as polished knives. This means war.

———

THE NEXT DAY, the injured quail is surprisingly still alive. Her food is scattered and her water bottle spilled; her bedding is soaked, and her sore bum is caked with a new thick layer of poop and bird food. She flaps her wings and digs her beak into the bedding. Her eyes are bright and clear, her energy level is high, and gentle touches to her exposed skin reveal no feverish heat of infection. She hasn't gotten worse; I can't justify putting her down. But her viability is still questionable, so I don't want to commit to healing and rehabilitating her. We'll keep her one more day, overnight, and see how she's doing the next morning.

I bathe her again, realizing that because she cannot walk, she is sitting in her own excrement like a baby in a dirty diaper. After reapplying soothing antiseptic cream to her hindquarters, I wrap her in a towel to dry and ask B to hold her while I clean and refurbish her hospital room.

———

OUTSIDE, I TEND to my quails, then refill the bird feeders and check the rat traps. The snap traps are empty beneath the tilted plastic bins that protect the other wild critters from their bone-breaking grasp, but the live trap again contains the squirrel. She looks exceptionally rotund today. When released, she darts away quickly, then a few seconds later reappears on the porch, looking about for the day's bowl of peanuts. She stands on her hind legs for a moment, and I notice that in addition to her round belly, her nipples are also protruding.

"I got you, Momma," I comment, as I set aside the peanut bowl in favor of a flat board upon which I scatter extra peanuts, a handful of sunflower seeds, and a pinch of dried mealworms. No pregnant lady should have to hoist herself into a shoulder-height bowl, and growing babies need extra food.

———————

ON THE SECOND day after the rat attack, despite the severity of her wounds, the little hen is still alive and shows no signs of infection. She drags herself about, awkwardly and clumsily, by flapping her wings and digging her beak into her bedding, her little legs trailing pathetically behind her.

Surprisingly, she is still eating and drinking. A critically injured animal will not have the energy to put toward such basic tasks and will fade quickly if not kept hydrated. But despite her handicap, she somehow manages to regularly dip her beak into her water trough and nibble on the scattered food.

She appears to be viable, but what quality of life can I expect her to have? Will she ever be able to walk again, or would she be sentenced to flopping about on an abrasive, wire-mesh pen floor, caked in her own poop and needing daily baths?

If she were a human, she would communicate, consent, contribute to the discussion. And if she were a human and wished for such, as many efforts and resources as possible would be put into her survival and recovery. But if she were disliked vermin, a rat, perhaps, she'd be euthanized. What if she were a beloved creature, perhaps a young family dog with a potential life span over twenty years, instead of a barnyard bird that could only reasonably live a few years. What value do we place on a creature when deciding whether it should live or die. And how much of that decision is made for our own comfort rather than for its well-being.

B tells me of the starfish piglets he knew in his childhood: stepped on by their clumsy mothers shortly after birth, these splay-legged, belly-crawling, helpless infants sometimes had paralyzing spinal fractures and needed to be put down. But sometimes, they just had temporary soft tissue damage, and, with quiet rest and gentle care, they would recover and lead normal lives. You didn't know which it was going to be until a week of bottle-feeding the babies and keeping them in a blanket-lined box in a warm kitchen.

I again bathe the bird and put her back in her cleaned hospital tub. I'll decide tomorrow whether to euthanize or try to nurse her back to health.

I repeat this routine and contemplation daily—for a week.

Within a few days, the quail's flesh wounds close, and her feathers begin to regrow. She can now lift her head and shoulders, and she scoots about on her beak and wings like an awkward crab or starfish scurrying across the ground. But her legs remain limp, useless.

Remembering the physiotherapy used on people recovering from spinal injuries and pelvic fractures, I spread an old towel on the kitchen table. I cup the bird in my hands with her legs dangling down below my fingers, then lower her until her feet are flat against the towel. I feel her tiny pelvic muscles flex, adjusting to the forgotten pressure. I hold her steady for a few seconds, until she starts to tremble, then lower her to the towel, her legs folded loosely beneath her, to rest. After a minute, I raise her again until her legs are supporting a bit of her weight and hold her steady. I repeat this muscle-strengthening exercise three or four times, until her legs no longer flex and cooperate.

The next morning after I wash her bum, I repeat the simple physiotherapy. And again, in the evening after dinner.

From one day to the next, the little hen grows stronger. The length of time she can stand up with my hands cupped around her grows exponentially longer—from a few seconds to ten, to a minute, to two minutes. She starts using her right foot to help propel herself as she flops about in her hospital tub.

On sunny afternoons, I take her outside and sit with her in my lap or set her down on the lawn beside me. She stretches her head up high, neck long and eyes wide, at the familiar sounds and smells. When I put her next to a clump of cut grass that escaped B's lawnmower, she flop-scoots over to it and buries herself, using her beak to pull grass over her back until only her little head is showing. She chirps contentedly in the sunlight.

After a week of simple physiotherapy, the hen can stand on her right leg and even take a step, but her left leg remains crippled and folded beneath her. If I cup my hand around her left side, she will lean on it and stand on both feet, but when I pull my hand away, she falls down. I poke at the bones of her pelvis gently and determine that her left hip was likely broken in the rat attack.

My own left hip was shattered in a car accident when I was sixteen and left to heal as-is without the support of implanted medical pins or a plaster cast. The next few months were a frustrating struggle of pain, disability, and gradually growing mobility. I can now stand and walk well, albeit with recurring soreness and the stiffness of arthritis creeping in—could this little bird eventually do so as well? Yet again, I wonder what quality of life this bird can be expected to achieve.

A VISITING FRIEND sits on the lawn with the quail and me. "What's her name?" she asks.

I think of a motivational video my high school classmates and I had to watch. Rescuing one stranded starfish by retrieving it from a dry beach and throwing it back into the ocean doesn't change the world, but it makes a world of difference to that one starfish. This tiny, needy quail is just another bland brown bird in my flock; she doesn't even have an interesting color pattern. The cost to replace her would not justify the amount of time and effort I put into taking care of her. It's not worth it to me.

But it is worth it to her.

"Starfish," I reply.

ON THE TWELFTH day after the rat attack, during the daily standing therapy, I notice that while Starfish's right foot stands flat and splay toed as normal, her left foot tends to curl up like a floppy fist so she is standing on the back of her wrist. I realize that, just as her leg muscles had atrophied as she healed and needed physiotherapy to work properly again, the muscles of her left foot had grown weak while she favored her broken limb.

I gather a handful of makeshift medical supplies—scissors, medical tape, a twist tie from a bag of produce—and enlist B's help. He holds her up as I bend the twist tie into a tiny splint and attach it to her weak foot with bits of medical tape. She cannot walk and is likely uncomfortable, but her leg and toes are now forced into a proper position.

After twenty-four hours, the splint is ragged and covered in poop. I remove it and place Starfish on the tabletop therapy towel.

She stands.

Only for a few moments before she flops onto her side, but—she stands, on both feet.

I scoop her up, then set her back down on the towel without touching her legs. Her left leg is weak, unable to support much weight, but her toes and ankles are all straight and in the proper position.

On the thirteenth and fourteenth days, I continue with her daily baths and physiotherapy.

On the fifteenth day, I open the hospital tub to find Starfish standing. She cocks her head sideways, peeking up at me with one bright eye, and chirps. I pick her up. Although it has been a half day since her last bumbath, her feathers and hindquarters are clean and free of sticky poop.

Setting her on the towel-covered tabletop, I examine her. Her wounds are healed and dry, and aside from a patch of new growing feathers, she looks like a normal, uninjured quail. She stands properly, on both feet. I nudge her, and she walks: she has a pronounced limp and flaps her wings for balance with every step. But she walks.

Relieved that this little near casualty has proven herself to be not only viable but mobile, I lean back in my chair and watch her hobble about.

She stops, bows as though about to do a happy hop—and flies off the table. Startled by the sudden, unfamiliar noise of flapping wings, the cat, who had been sitting on the windowsill watching butterflies, leaps from her perch and bolts away down the hall. I rush to grab Starfish and put her back in her hospital bin. This animal's critical needs—medical care, cleanliness, and quiet isolation—have been taken care of and no longer need to be addressed. Now, it is time to address her secondary needs: home, companionship, and intellectual stimulation.

I gather up my other surviving quails and tuck them temporarily into their lidded plastic bins on the porch. The hens chirp and burble; Stinker crows incessantly, aghast at being thusly confined and unable to strut about proudly.

After rearranging the quail pen's furnishings, I place Starfish in its center and leave her to reorient herself. Fluttering her wings as she hobble-walks, she pecks at the food, skitters back and forth through a PVC tube several times, then awkwardly hoists herself into the sand tray for a long-overdue, refreshing sand bath.

An hour later, I return the other quails to the pen: first the mellowest hens, then the more aggressive ones, then Stinker. The flock acts no different than any other time I have returned them to their pen after cleaning and moving it. It is difficult to gauge quails' social interactions unless something goes wrong or there is obvious conflict; today, they either ignore Starfish or accept her.

THE PREGNANT SQUIRREL disappears for a few days, then reappears: smaller, slimmer, and voraciously hungry. Instead of our usual offering of a handful of peanuts per day, we give her as much food as she wants. Two, sometimes three times per day, she perches on our porch, ravenously eating one mouthful after another: peanuts, birdseed, sunflower seeds, whatever nuts we have on hand. In her pre-motherhood days, she would gather any extra food and hide it, piling it in an empty birdhouse or burying it in the lawn—but now, she has no time for such shenanigans. She has nursing babies to feed.

When sitting on the porch, I take to cupping a few seeds in my palm and resting my hand on the table or dangling it loosely beside me. At first, the squirrel is hesitant, grabbing a seed, then darting away. Within a few days, however, she becomes confident, resting her little front paws on my fingers as she selects her next morsel. I close my seed-filled hand into a loose fist, and she shoves her head into it. Her fur is smooth and soft, and her whiskers feel like dandelion fluff.

A MONTH AFTER Starfish is reintegrated back into the flock, I again find the quails quiet and huddled, crammed together in a back corner of the pen, their water bottles knocked over and food strewn about. At the center of the cage lies one dead bird: wings akimbo, bloody neck stretched long, eyes closed.

A rat. Again. *But how did it get in?* The cage has been reinforced, the wire mesh affixed to the thick wood frame with enough hardware staples to stock a building supplies store.

Peering into the corner opposite from the huddled quails, I find a small stretch of wire mesh that is bowed out from the wood, forming a rat-sized hole. A half-dozen loose staples are scattered on the cage floor beneath it; a few more are dangling from the loose wire. The rat, clever and determined, must have slammed its body aggressively against the pen wall again and again to push loose all those staples.

Borrowing B's staple gun, I close the hole with a solid row of staples, nailing a strip of plywood over it for extra security, then stomp over to the house to complain to B about the persistently bloodthirsty vermin.

B does what he always does when there's a problem that could be addressed by designing a solution. He does what he always does: he disappears.

He disappears into his workshop.

At first, there is relative quiet, just the muffled babble of a *CBC Radio* talk show. Then, there is cacophony: the banging of a hammer, the squeal and thump of an electric saw, the gunshot crack of a nail gun, all occasionally punctuated by more shouted curses in Latverian.

For several days, I see little of B. He occasionally appears in the house, covered in sawdust-sticky sweat and smelling like a dead goat, to eat or use the washroom. The aural warfare continues well into the night: when it peaks, I half expect smoke to rise from the workshop's roof or for an electric breaker to blow. In a quieter moment, from the corner of my eye, I glimpse the bright flash of an arc welder.

B ASSEMBLES THE new quail pen on the lawn. Built from thick pieces of wood and heavier wire mesh, it is too sturdy for the coyotes to tear into and too solid and precise in detail for the rats to forcefully shove their way into. The door is double latched so that even a creature that scratches and manages to knock one of its locks free will not be able to gain entrance. The wooden roof is hinged so it can be opened to allow ease of movement while cleaning and reorganizing the pen.

But it is huge: ten feet wide, ten feet deep, and nearly as tall as I am. If the first quail pen was challenging to move to a fresh spot on the lawn every month, how are we going to handle this one?

Grinning, B points out a design feature: the pen has wheels. On two corners of the pen are small axels upon which large, removable rubber tires can be placed. On the opposite side, a long handle spans the pen's width. B snaps the wheels into place. Grabbing the handle, we lift in tandem and propel the pen around the yard like a giant wooden wheelbarrow. We set the pen on a patch of grass that has not yet been fertilized by quail poop and pop the wheels off. Gathering the furnishings from the old pen, I wash them off with the hose and set to interior decorating.

Alarmed by the sudden emptiness of their home, the quails run around frantically, then huddle in a corner. Stinker stands apart from them, yelling fowl language.

"You'll like your new home," I assure them, but they just stare at me blankly. Apparently, inbred farm poultry have little capacity for insight or gratitude.

One at a time, I carry the quails over to their new pen and place them inside: first wobbly Starfish, then the other hens, then the rooster. Unaccustomed to moving across a distance without actively walking, the carried birds twitch their legs and bob their heads, pigeon-like, as I walk.

As I place Stinker in the new pen, I notice a large plastic plug embedded in the pen's wall near the ground.

"That's for the habiquail," B declares in an insufferably smug tone, then refuses to explain further.

It is impossible to tell whether the quails realize they are in a different home. They seem happy, or at least content: they chirp and burble nearly constantly, Stinker occasionally crowing over his domain, while running through tubes, attacking bugs and their food dish, and snoozing in sunbeams. There are so few of them compared to the capacity of this big cage, though. They are like a small handful of marbles rolling around in a huge wooden bowl.

The novelty of raising quail chicks has faded: They are adorable, but we have had quite enough of our house smelling like poultry poop from birds kept in a bin in the spare room. So, I buy a half-dozen hens from a local farmer and integrate them into the flock. Stinker and his wives do or do not notice. Their little bright eyes reveal no emotion or thought processes.

I didn't intend to keep birds. Now, I have many.

The sun rises and sets. The quails chirp and lay ridiculously tiny eggs. The bees hum and gather nectar. Between moments of inhabiting the live trap, the squirrel skitters across the porch and demands more peanuts. The rooster crows.

LIFE ADVICE FROM BIRB

- If an object is smaller than your face, you should try to eat it.

- Poop often. Wherever you are, whatever you're doing, poop.

- Bathe frequently, thoroughly, and enthusiastically. Disregard your resulting appearance.

- Stand on your food, especially if it's presented on a dish. It feels nice on your feet, and you can move your toes around in it and even sleep on it if you want.

- Remember to poop.

- Blink with your bottom eyelids. Why be like everyone else. Be unique in small ways. People will find it cute.

- Talk to yourself all the time. This will entice others to pay attention to you.

- If you're feeling bad (hungry, lonely, scared), yell. Someone will come by and pat you or give you a dish of food to stand on.

- Fly. Even if you can't or are terrible at it, try. There is no substitute for enthusiasm.

THE DOOR OF the live trap is shut. Something is banging about inside it and chewing on its bars. Expecting to release yet another bunny or the squirrel, or perhaps a particularly aggressive bird, I crouch down beside it and see—a rat.

Finally, we have caught one of the murderous vermin that slaughtered Birb and my other quails and injured Starfish, one of the pests that stalk and attack the wild birds. B will be pleased to know we can finally get some vengeance, as limited and belated as it may be.

Instead of continuing to thrash about in frustration and terror—or cowering in a corner away from me as any small, trapped wild animal would when facing an unknown, giant twolegs—the rat becomes still.

I stand up and start walking toward the house to tell B there is a rat that needs to be euthanized. But when I turn my back, the rat shrieks and resumes thrashing about.

Returning to the cage, I crouch back down. The rat quietens and looks up at me, her beady eyes steady and little nose twitching. I stand up slowly, maintaining eye contact. Instead of cowering or moving farther away from me, she scurries to the nearest corner and stands on her hind legs, her tiny paws resting on the bars of the trap. I turn and take a few steps away. The rat screams.

I crouch down by the cage again. The rat trots over and stands up like a little man, paws gripping the bars. She sticks her nose out and sniffs at me, runs the length of the trap and back, then stands up again, looking altogether like a patient prisoner peering out from between the bars of their cell.

Her ears are ragged and swollen from parasitic mites. One of her front paws is missing a finger.

Lifting the live trap by its handle, I stand up and carry the cage to the porch. Surprisingly, the rat does not panic or thrash about; she simply crouches on the floor of the cage, her bright eyes fixated on me. I set the trap on the porch. The rat stares at me. I step away from the trap. The rat screams.

After listening to my blow-by-blow recounting of my encounter with the rat, B sighs and curses in Latverian, then wipes a tear from his cheek. Hardened hearts break easily.

Any murderous creature that slaughters our little family members should be killed, both as punishment and as protective measure. But any being—person or creature—that cries for help should be saved. And anyone with a heart could understand what that terrified creature was saying.

We load the live trap—wrapped in an old towel to minimize the spread of rat feces and parasites—into the back of the car and drive to a forested park a few miles away. The trap is set down on the grass. Its door is opened. The rat scurries out and away.

AFTER ANOTHER NOISY afternoon in the workshop, B emerges carrying a smaller, doghouse-sized version of the new quail pen and a piece of PVC pipe. He sets the little pen beside the quail pen, removes the mysterious round plastic plug from the pen's wall, slides the end of the pipe into the hole, attaches the other end of the pipe to the little pen, and stands back proudly.

"It's a habiquail," he says, grinning at his pun.

I doubt my birds' ability to discover their new pen without assistance. Stepping inside the pen, I grab a bird and stuff them into the tube to the habiquail. The quail runs through the tube and freezes, finding themself in an entirely new space.

Picking up each of the other birds, I insert them into the portal. At their exit, the birds shove into each other and freeze, stunned and staring, piling up like an inconvenient crowd of pedestrians at the bottom of a relentless escalator.

The flock fits into the habiquail—barely. After several minutes of mute shock, one bird chirps and goes back into the tube. Another follows, then another, popping out into the main pen—then they turn and return to the habiquail. For the next half hour, the quails wander back and forth between the two pens, exploring, playing, learning. I wonder what their perception of space is, how they interpret this new extension of their home. When they look out through the wired walls of the habiquail, do they recognize the exterior of the main pen due to the birds and furnishings within it? What is their understanding of where they are, of where they have been?

WE CATCH ANOTHER rat in the live trap. Then another. After a dozen, I stop counting. A small youngling cowers in a corner of the trap. A battle-scarred male with huge, dragging testicles lunges at the trap's walls. A massive pregnant female waddles from one end of the trap to the other. An old rat with patchy fur and mite-crusted ears tries desperately to wriggle out through the bars of the trap. Sometimes, we catch two in a day; sometimes, nothing for months.

Each rat is dutifully relocated to the forested park where it may or may not find its repatriated family members. The females will likely be accepted into whatever colony of rats is already living there. The males might not, unless they are quite young or recognized by the others. B is relieved that he does not have to repeatedly execute these furry little creatures with their clever minds. The rats are likely ignorant and ungrateful for our consideration. They are smart creatures but have no way of knowing that they could have been killed.

SUMMER FADES AGAIN into autumn, then winter. B nails homemade storm windows to the quail pen, and I remove the habiquail until spring. I wait in trepidation for the rats to again attack the pen in search of rare winter food. Will the reinforced pen hold up to their attacks? Will I lose more quails?

My stomach drops when I see a small pile of dirt outside the edge of the quail pen. I peer inside the pen—but my birds are fine, uninjured and behaving normally.

Visible beneath the wire-mesh floor, however, is a long, snaking rat tunnel. It opens into a larger space, the size of my spread hand, below the heat lamp.

The rats are unable to catch the birds now, but of course they'd still take advantage of the pen's warmth and shelter. I have found similar rat tunnels when I've moved the paver stones by the porch or removed the protective plastic sheeting from my garden beds in the spring. Under the quail cage, the rats would have access to whatever food the quails spilled and threw about, and they could try to grab a random egg or bird foot within reach.

I pour shovelfuls of sand through the wire floor, filling the tunnel, and set the live trap beside the quail pen. The next day, we have yet another rat to relocate. And a week later, another sub-floor tunnel appears beneath the pen's wire bottom.

Even if we caught or killed every rat on the property, within a few weeks, they'd be replaced by rodents from the farm down the road or the neighbor's garage. Filling the rat tunnels with sand and dirt becomes a regular part of my poultry winter care.

A FEW HENS die each year from old age, ailments caused by inbreeding, or hidden injury and infection. Laying eggs every day is physically exhausting work and takes its toll on their tiny bodies. I bury them alongside their predecessors under the rhododendron bush, but I do not replace them. I did not intend to keep poultry, and when the last of the birds passes on, I will have poultry no more.

One winter, my flock dwindles down to one bedraggled hen and Stinker. They are often together: cuddled up in the sand bath, sitting side by side under the heat lamp, or eating from the food trough in tandem.

The hen grows weak and frail. She wobbles when she walks and has little energy. In any other situation, I would cull her—but she is Stinker's only companion. And even if I intended to replace her, poultry are plentiful in the marketplace during the warm seasons, but in winter, they are challenging to find.

On a blustery, gray afternoon, I find the little hen lying stiff and cold. Stinker is crouched loyally beside her. He looks up at me, bold and unblinking, and crows a quiet *whatthefuck*.

I leave him to mourn over his last wife while I dig her grave in the hard, wet soil.

When I reach into the pen to remove her, I cover Stinker with my other hand, gently ruffling his feathers and blocking his view.

I return to give Stinker fresh water and an extra-large handful of dried mealworms. He is still crouched in the same spot. *Whatthefuck*, he mumbles unenthusiastically.

STINKER CROWS EVERY few minutes, all day, and through most of the night. For weeks. He is calling for his flock. He is calling for his wives. He is calling for his friends and, getting no answer, keeps calling.

Stinker is an old boy; he has lived nearly twice as long as I had expected him to. I did not intend to keep quails, and now I am back to having only one. I'd be surprised if he survived this winter. I briefly consider euthanizing him, then dismiss the idea. Killing an apparently healthy animal because he is inconvenient or undesired would be selfish. If he survives the winter, I decide, I will get him a few hens to keep him company in his old age.

———

WHEN THE FIRST flowers of spring bloom, I reach out to a local farmer who raises quails for the grocery industry. His roosters are butchered young for their meat; his hens produce eggs that he gathers and sells by the case. When his hens grow old or stop laying, they are culled and rendered into pet food.

"Do you have some old hens I can buy off you?" I ask. "The older the better. It's okay if they've stopped laying."

I do not wish to purchase young birds in case they end up outliving senior Stinker by years, and I end up in the same situation again. The farmer sells me a handful of hens that are no longer laying and are earmarked for the butcher's block.

The birds are surprisingly quiet on the drive home. They neither chirp nor run around in their box nor leap up and smack against its top.

I place Stinker in a storage bin, move and rearrange the quail pen, and place the hens inside. They huddle together, still and silent, their eyes wide. Half-bald and bedraggled, their backs pebbly stretches of bare skin, they have so few feathers I cannot discern what colors they are.

These birds had been kept in minimalistic three-square-foot cages since chickhood. Like any animals raised in an industrial-agricultural setting, their accommodations were simple and sufficient but not luxurious, oftentimes viewed as harsh and heartless, designed for high productivity and short lifespans. To keep them in settings that promoted their best well-being, acknowledged their natural tendencies, and nurtured their psychologies would be expensive for the farmer and result in higher market prices. Although it would be preferable for the entire agricultural industry to follow higher standards, doing so would result in only wealthy people having access to nutritious food. There is a constant struggle for balance: between our own well-being and that of the animals we keep for our uses.

These birds have lived in tiny, crowded cages in a barn their entire adult lives. They have never felt the ground beneath their feet, fresh wind on their feathers, or been touched by sunlight. They don't know what the world sounds like without the constant hum of an industrial fan clearing ammonia and dust from their air. The foreign grass, strange-smelling atmosphere, and alien sounds of the surrounding wild birds and trees are likely overwhelming, if not terrifying. And they don't know how to move about in such a huge space, where they can walk freely without bumping into each other.

In his bin on the porch, Stinker crows exasperatedly. I leave him there for an exceptionally long handful of hours as the hens slowly disperse and cautiously explore their new surroundings. When I finally return him to the pen, he stands very still for a moment, then runs around excitedly, burbling and clucking.

As the sun dips low and turns the air dusky and pink, the hens gather along the west side of the pen and face the outdoors: necks stretched long, eyes wide and focused, so still they are barely breathing. They have never before seen a sunset or a sunrise. They don't know what is happening. They don't know if this world is ending or if the sun will rise again.

OVER THE NEXT few weeks, the bedraggled hens gradually regrow their feathers. Some of them are common brown with gold speckles like Stinker, or gold with brown speckles like Birb, but two are a beautiful snowy white with black spots. One has a chronic limp from a congenital deformity or ill-healed injury. Another is prone to fits of anxious squawking and random panic, her disposition likely the result of some neurological trauma.

The hens are allegedly barren, old, and beyond their egg-laying capability, but I am mildly unsurprised when, one day, I find a pale-blue egg, as perfect and pretty as a robin's, in the quail pen. Happy animals living in an entertainment-rich mansion and supplementing their dry-kibble diet with natural bugs and grass and veggies from a garden are more likely to have healthy, functioning reproductive systems than ones kept in minimal enclosures.

After several days of producing the wonky eggs that typify a young or newly restarted uterus—dark, round eggs; tiny, yolkless fairy eggs; squishy, shell-less eggs; huge, oblong, double-yolked eggs streaked with blood; eggs with pale-green shells—the hens settle into a regular routine of each laying one egg per day. As though they had never stopped. As though they had always had beetle snacks, and dust baths, and wind on their feathers, and sunsets.

THE LIVE TRAP snaps like a tinny gunshot. Perhaps we've caught another rabbit, or a bird. Perhaps it is a rat that we'll have to relocate. Perhaps it is another of our fluffy-tailed tree rats: the feisty squirrel that steals seeds from my hand and climbs my skirt to get to her food, or her overgrown adult son whom she chastises and chases away, or one of the large, invasive gray squirrels that frequently try to raid the bird feeders.

Whether food or traps, anything set out to entice wildlife must be monitored and maintained. A bird feeder kept stocked all summer and fall cannot be allowed to run dry or empty in the winter lest the birds that have come to rely on it starve. A trap set to capture or kill a pest or predator must be watched and dealt with lest its occupant be tortured and suffer unnecessarily. These creatures are the smallest things in our lives and do not need us to survive, but they come to rely on us, and that is a responsibility we must respect.

THE QUAILS CHATTER and coo as they wander about in their havenly enclosure, scurrying through their PVC tunnels and flopping about in their dust-bath sandbox. I often see one or two of them staring out the screened walls, transfixed by some motion or light in the yard beyond. They make no move to escape when I open the door. I wonder how far a distance their eyes can focus, what concept they have of the world outside their pen.

When a neighbor's dog lunges playfully at the pen, or the shadow of an eagle flying overhead comes near, the quails rush to a far corner and hide or crouch down and freeze, their eyes wide and unblinking. They are so small and so vulnerable—they are protected in their home, but they don't know they are safe.

On mild nights when the air is warm and calm, while the flock snoozes inside their bulletproof pen, there is often one hen or another alone in the habiquail, sitting quietly with her feet tucked under her. Her little dark eyes reflect starlight, and the moon, and the distant neighbor's porch lights.

Three Grams

A TINY HUMMINGBIRD SITS on the lawn, a multicolored iridescent spot against the grass and weeds. Hummingbirds are not ground birds. They have tiny legs and cannot walk. They live in the trees and bushes and the air, perching on branches, flying. Something is wrong.

In afternoon sunlight, large windows on houses become mirrors reflecting the trees and sky, obscuring the house's contents. Wild birds don't understand glass or mirrors. They understand sky and trees and react accordingly, flying through the air until they crash, suddenly, into something invisible, creating a distinct thump and leaving a soft halo of feathers stuck to the glass. The bird falls, shocked and concussed, or neckbroke and dead, onto the ground below.

I wrap the hummingbird in my hand to keep him warm against the chill of shock and protected against opportunistic predators. He weighs no more than a small coin.

This isn't the first time I've held a hummingbird. As a teenager, I sat on the porch holding a window-bonked hummer for an hour, shooing away three hungry cats and two curious dogs, until the little bird recovered from her misadventure. When she began to move and look around, I fed her sugar water from a bottle cap until she perked up, flew in a circle, and perched on my finger. She preened her feathers back into place before finally buzzing away. She was so light and small that my skin didn't even register her weight, the poke of her tiny claws.

But today, there are no feathers stuck to our window, and I'd heard no tragic thump against the glass. This little guy had encountered some unknown misfortune: another house's window, perhaps, or a car, a predator, or some poison a neighbor had set out to battle the moles and rats that subvert his postcard-perfect lawn.

The bird does not perk up even after I give him sugar water and a long rest in my hand. Without known history or visible injury, I am uncertain of his viability. I furnish a small cardboard box with a soft cloth and a tray of sugar water, gently place the hummer in it, fold the lid shut, and set it in the spare room, closing the door against our curious house pets.

In the morning, we will open the box containing Schrödinger's bird, then either dig the tiniest grave, or load the bird in his box into the car and drive an hour to the wild animal rescue center for medical care, or set the recovered animal free. Nature is hard and cruel and beautiful, but sometimes, it surprises us.

Schrödinger's Sting

THERE ARE MANY moments of standing still for long stretches, staring off into the unfocused distance with heels resting on the earth, a few strands of hair blowing across the face, breathing quietly, thinking. Sometimes, the goings-on inside one's head are so complex, so profound that the eyes unfocus, the mind lifts and spreads across a widening space, and the body stops moving.

If the urban sprawl of the local cities continues, what will a satellite photo of the area look like in a few decades. If a square-inch plug of sweetgrass will grow to two feet in diameter within a year, and I have sixteen square feet of sweetgrass plants that could be split up and replanted, how long would it take to cover a whole acre. If bees fly up to five miles to forage, and we're three miles from the country's border, how many people in the next country can reasonably consider our backyard honey to be local. If I move my legs, or let go of the fistful of clothing clutched in my hand, will the wasp or bee that's caught in the elastic of my underwear sting me?

I WAS NOODLING around the garden with no particular goal, as I often do on sunny afternoons, in a long cotton skirt, light shirt, and wide-brimmed hat. I pulled the occasional weed, guided a sprawling bean plant back up its wire climbing rack, checked under zucchini leaves for aphids. I poked the baby squashes to check for blossom-end rot; any that were soft and withering I twisted off and lobbed into the forest.

It was a movie-perfect afternoon: The warm sun made the fluffy clouds glow yellow-white, and songbirds twittered and flew in the trees and around the bird feeders. The beehives were humming: in front of each, a cloud of forager bees swooped in figure eights to orient themselves before heading out to gather pollen and nectar. The sound of the hives was soothing background music, like the purring of thousands of tiny kittens, and the occasional gust of breeze brought me the soft, sweet scent of beeswax and ripening honey. Somewhere on the back end of the property, a squirrel staccato barked, seeking a mate or warning off rivals.

I was careful, while wandering through my garden, to not step on the soaker hose I'd wound between the plants so it could ooze water nonstop to their roots. On warm afternoons, such damp objects attract honey bees—and the occasional wasp—that line up like tiny patrons at a pub bar, drinking and collecting water to take back to their hives. The drinking bees pay no mind to large intruders and will even tolerate a gentle fingerpat on their fuzzy backs. They're busy working and have no hive beside them to defend, so a bump or brush is as ignored by them as a tap from a fluttering leaf. But I do not wish to disturb their work, or to accidentally crush them with a clumsy foot, so I am always careful to not step on the bees and their watering hole hose. When I crouch down to pull a weed or harvest a few tomatoes, I make sure my long skirt is tucked closely around my legs and not inadvertently draped over the hose. It would not do for a bee to finish gathering water, try to fly off, and get tangled in the tent of my skirt next to my vulnerably bare legs.

One of the sunflowers was leaning precariously and needed to be propped up. My sunflowers grow a magnificent twelve feet or taller, sometimes to an immeasurable height that overlooks the roof of the house, and as their heads grow huge and heavy with seeds, they tend to slouch and lean. B has built me a tall rack of poles and rope that I can lash the sunflower stalks to, but the ropes need periodic adjustment as the plants' aggressive growth pulls them up and toward the path of the sun.

Adjusting the sunflower's ropes was a minor task, but the spot I needed to reach was slightly above my head. I stepped onto the narrow, foot-high wooden edge of the garden bed, one hand braced against the sunflower rack for balance, and tugged at the rope until the leaning plant settled securely upright against the rack. I stepped back and down off the wooden plot edge, tugging my skirt as it tangled between my knees.

And felt a familiar, sharp pain, like a staple slammed into my skin by my hipbone.

Impulsively, I grabbed at the spot where I felt the sting, clenching a thick fistful of skirt and underwear and squeezing it tight to contain and crush whatever stung me.

And then I froze.

A stinging insect—bee or wasp, I had no way of knowing—had inadvertently flown up my skirt as I fussed with the sunflower. And as I stepped down, it had gotten pinched in the soft fold of flesh between my belly and upper thigh and had reacted to this sudden threat by stinging.

In quantum mechanics, there is a thought experiment commonly known as Schrödinger's cat. Physicist Erwin

Schrödinger described a hypothetical situation in which a cat is shut in a box with a vial of poison that may or may not crack open, instantly killing the cat. After some time has passed, has the cat been killed by the poison and in need of a burial, or is the cat still alive and in need of food? The box is unmovable and soundproof; there is no way to observe the cat and see if they are still breathing or not.

Common sense says that, of course, the cat is either alive or dead; it cannot be both. But in terms of quantum mechanics and practical planning, until you open the box and see for yourself, the cat is both alive *and* dead.

Within my clenched hand was now a wadded fistful of fabric—underwear and skirt—that may or may not include a stinging insect that might or might not sting me again. Or the insect—alive and now angry or dead and thus harmless—was somewhere else, free within the billows of my skirt. And within the area of navel to knee, there are body parts that I definitely do not want to have stung.

———

BEEKEEPING IS A profession with a badass reputation.

Beekeeping is badass—but that reputation implies not only facing a certain amount of danger but also a blasé or nonchalant attitude regarding said danger. Courage is not facing something other people are afraid of; courage is facing something you yourself are afraid of.

Your friends may not know that you spend hours under the blinding-hot sun, salty sweat stinging your eyes and the heat pounding your head, lifting forty-pound boxes while wearing a heavy canvas suit, thick leather gloves, and tall boots in midsummer heat. But they know you could get stung. They may not know that you have to make life-or-death decisions about thousands or millions of living creatures, diagnosing and triaging ailing colonies and faltering queens, choosing what treatments and methodologies to administer, who to save, who to just leave alone, and when to euthanize. But they know you could get stung. And they know that bees are imperative for human survival and the well-being of the ecology; beekeepers are people who have chosen a profession centered on stewarding, shepherding, and protecting bees. And they know you could get stung.

Thus, beekeeping is seen as a pastime that is noble, admirable, and courageous. Beekeepers are people who do this important and potentially dangerous work with dignity, grace, and dedication. Beekeeping is badass.

HONEY BEES STING once, then die. Wasps can sting multiple times and survive.

Bee stingers are modified ovipositors, retractable tubes that are used by females to deposit eggs. Male bees—drones—do not have stingers. They have rigid, pointed penises with serrated, fishhook-like barbs on their sides. This organ serves one single purpose and cannot be used to injure or defend. Thus, I often handle drones without consequence: cupping them in a hand for close inspection, cuddling them like tiny puppies, or gently tucking one between two fingers and placing it on the arm of an unsuspecting and easily startled friend.

In female Western honey bees, the ovipositor has evolved into a weapon of defense, a hollow needle that injects a toxic fluid. A healthy hive has tens of thousands of female worker bees, each of which only lives a few weeks, so the loss of a few bees who died defending their queen and hive is of no great consequence; ergo, the suicidal barbs on the workers' stingers have not been lost with evolution. A worker bee stings once, her stinger remains impaled in the tough human flesh, she tears away, and she dies.

Certain wasps and hornets, on the other hand, have colonies that are much smaller and more impacted by the loss of a few members. Unlike their vegetarian pollinator cousins—the honey bees who eat primarily nectar and pollen—wasps and hornets are aggressive predators. They hunt and eat mosquitoes, bugs, flies, and the larvae and caterpillars of other insects. It would be illogical for one to die while killing a prey they intend to consume or to carry back to its nest. Thus, their stingers have evolved to be barbless, smooth as sewing needles, and reusable. A European hornet or yellow jacket wasp—common creatures throughout North America—can sting multiple times without consequence to itself.

Thus, the magnitude of danger of the situation I'm in depends on whether the creature that is caught in my underwear and has stung me is a wasp or a honey bee.

If a bee, then there is no danger in releasing my grip on the skirt and underwear clenched in my fist, possibly containing a small, buzzing creature. It has already stung me in the relatively neutral area of my hip bone, and what I hold could be a now-defenseless, disemboweled, dying insect. But if a wasp, then opening my hand could release a furious and now further-angered creature that could sting again, even several times. Or if my hand holds only fabric, then the wasp is still somewhere on or in my underclothing, and any movement of my skirt or legs could be perceived as a threat or attack that would provoke further self-defense.

I stand there, immobile, pondering the possibilities and how to proceed.

THE MOMENT OF being stung feels like being poked with a sewing needle or thumbtack. A sting that hits a sensitive spot feels like slamming a staple into your flesh. There is a short, sharp pain followed by a visceral shiver throughout the body. A dull ache follows in the area that was stung: with bee stings, the ache fades within a few minutes, but with wasp or hornet stings, the pain can persist for days.

Within a day, any swelling may stretch the skin and irritate the nerves, causing a relentless itch as the body fights off the toxin. If not infected or exacerbated by scratching, within a day or two, the swelling begins to recede, and the irritating itching abates.

I am glad I do not have allergies or extreme sensitivities. Some people's immune systems overreact to bee venom, which can result in such extreme swelling that within minutes or hours, the body's ability to breathe or keep internal organs functioning is critically impeded. Immediate medical attention is imperative to save the person's life. Bee venom allergies are not something to second-guess. And such allergies are generally discovered through an emergency situation.

The worst sting I ever had swelled my foot until I couldn't don a sock or shoe for days. Another puffed up half my face grotesquely, one eye squeezed shut until only the very tips of my eyelashes were visible. But such reactions are merely uncomfortable inconveniences, not life-threatening reactions—I am part of the 94 percent of the human population that are not currently allergic to bees. For now. Among the general population, it is rare for someone to randomly become allergic to bee venom, but among beekeepers, 32 percent will experience an extreme reaction or develop a life-threatening allergy due to long-term exposure to it. But I am not worried by this possibility. We keep emergency medication on hand, and I know what symptoms are worthy of concern.

I AM STANDING in my garden with a wad of skirt, underwear, and potentially a stinging bug clenched in my fist. If it were entangled in my hat or glove, I could simply remove the accessory—but one's underclothing is not such a simple matter. I am accustomed to being stung on the hand or face, but nether regions are far more sensitive areas. And unless I could determine where this unknown creature is after I release it, any movement made from the waist down could trigger further stinging.

ASKING A BEEKEEPER whether they have been stung is like asking a woodworker if they ever get a sliver or a chef if they ever scald their fingers on a hot pan. There are those who claim they have never had such an injury. And then there are those who tell the truth.

During the beekeeping season of spring through fall, it is a rare month that I don't get stung. With proper protective gear in good repair, it is unlikely that one will get stung often, but sometimes, bees find their way through a poorly closed zipper, or they get riled up and aim for a thin spot in the fabric, or the bees seem calm so you go gloveless, but you accidentally trap a bee between your fingers and it zaps you. You get used to such things, though they still hurt.

Getting stung while working directly with beehives is generally a result of equipment malfunction or user error—my hand fumbles and drops a frame and angers the bees, I forget the gloves inside the house and decide to go forth and risk it without them, a faulty zipper pops open without notice.

But getting stung in other situations is generally just poor luck and timing, flesh and bee meeting in an unintended manner. I once tiptoed barefoot across the lawn to retrieve an empty hummingbird feeder and stepped on a bee. A bee hitchhiked on the zipper pull of my astronaut suit and got pinched as I disrobed. A stray bee buzzed around the room and landed on the back of my knee while I was preparing frames of honeycomb for extraction; when I crouched down to adjust my shoes, the bee got trapped. While tidying up beekeeping tools that were left outside, I grabbed a honey-coated hive tool and inadvertently palmed a bee that was nibbling on the honey. Frequently, we unknowingly bring a handful of bees into the house on a bucket of honey or piece of beekeeping gear; if not noticed by sound or the behavior of the house pets, they are sometimes inadvertently found by a bare foot or ignorant hand.

I have lost count of the times I have been stung.

The corpses of bees must be picked up carefully between thumb and fingertips, not swept with the side of an open hand. The stinger of a dead bee is like a cocked rifle held by a fallen soldier: mishandling can result in injury. Even cleaning out the detritus at the bottom of the sink after washing beekeeping tools must be done carefully, for amidst the organic gunk and junk there may be a bee, half-drowned or dead, that could get wedged under a fingernail or prick the soft webbing of flesh between thumb and forefinger.

Even a stinger that has been separated from its bee—ripped out while stinging a person or broken off during postmortem damage—can give a painful jab, though it will only cause swelling if the yellowish venom sac is still attached. Thus, a stinger removed from the skin after a bee sting should be carefully thrown away before it gets caught in skin or clothing again, and I must be mindful to watch my hands while cleaning beekeeping equipment lest the tiny sliver of a bee-less stinger pokes into my fingers.

We beekeepers have our alarming adventures, of course. One memorable afternoon, we were removing frames of honeycomb from the hives for extraction and several dozen disapproving bees found a hole in my poorly affixed veil. I ran across the yard in a panic, a halo of angry bees accompanying me—B was close behind, yelling at me to stand still and smacking my head with his big hands to crush the bees inside my veil before they could sting me.

Occasionally, when one of us gets a bee inside our suit, the illogical panic response overtakes us. The bee-afflicted person drops their hive tool and runs away from the hives, tearing off their veil and suit in a frantic effort to dislodge the bee before it stings. Despite the crushing midsummer heat, we wear modest underwear instead of naked skin under our astronaut suits, for on any given day, we may end up disrobing on the lawn.

B often inspects the hives without gloves; he works cautiously and carefully, but it is not unusual to hear him bellow a string of colorful words when a random bee attacks his bare hands. It is pointless to try to retaliate against a stinging bee by poking or stinging it back—but it is certainly considered acceptable to yell at it.

Our neighbors and local pedestrians likely have interesting opinions on beekeeping—and the personalities of beekeepers—due to our antics. Most of the time, we work calmly, waving and smiling at passersby who stop to watch or ask a question. But sometimes, we can be observed yelling profanities, running around the yard tearing off our clothes, or punching each other. The passersby keep their distance. Beekeeping is badass, but you don't want to get too close to it.

IF I WERE alone and isolated, I could simply tear my skirt and underwear down and off in one motion, toss it away from me, sweep my hands across my nether regions to dislodge any stinging bug, and run half-naked around the side of the house and in through the door. But given my location, the timing would have to be impeccably perfect—at any moment, a car or bicycle could pass by, or the neighbor could glance through his window and witness my em-bare-ass-ment. How important is dignity to me?

We're already known as the weird house in the neighborhood, with our rusting yard sculptures, controversial rainbow flag, and roadside, public cupboard of free books. The locals are accustomed to seeing us undertaking mysterious tasks while garbed in big white astronaut suits, including occasionally frantically tearing off said suits. From their perspective, would they think it notable or odd to see one of the beekeepers running across the yard naked from the waist down, or would they assume it was just more evidence of our dedicated work ethic? Beekeeping is, after all, badass.

AT LEAST ONCE a year, an acquaintance or honey customer tells me they are allergic to bees. They look a bit sad, almost guilty. I ask them if they've ever been rushed to the hospital and treated for an allergic reaction to a sting and if they have a prescription for emergency antihistamines. They say yes to one or both quietly, as though they were disclosing a weakness or personal failing.

"You are strong," I say. "The immune system is the army that defends your body from harmful invaders like bacteria and viruses that may otherwise kill it. *Your* immune system is so responsive that it even overreacts to certain relatively harmless substances. It over-functions. Your immune system is twitchy and hyperaware; it is so protective of you that it practically has anxiety."

Some people smile brightly while telling me they are allergic to bees, almost as though it were a point of pride. When I ask if they've been taken to the hospital by ambulance after being stung, received an emergency prescription for stings, experienced an anaphylactic reaction to a sting, or if they have a blood relative who has, they say no, then tell me a story from their childhood.

Once upon a time when they were quite small, they were running in the park or playing in the yard, and a bee landed on them or stung them. The adults panicked; the child cried. It was very frightening. Ever since that incident, they have avoided bees, because bees sting.

I ask what the symptoms of their allergic reactions are, and they describe the common symptoms of a normal reaction. I tell them that their reactions sound similar to what happens to me when I get stung. I tell them that I am definitely not allergic.

They pause and look confused, as though I'd just told them fire wasn't hot. This information doesn't fit with their understanding of the world.

As cognitive beings, we tend to disapprove of strong emotions that are not rooted in a logical explanation. We are inclined to justify our reactions by providing reasons. It is not enough to be afraid of the dark, of the night, of the deep water; we invent monsters that inhabit it to give ourselves something specific to be afraid of. It is not enough to have had a frightening experience involving a bee; for the terror of such an experience to be justifiable, it must have been life-threatening.

IF PAIN WERE a color, a sting would be a small white flash with a dark line in the center. The bright dims quickly, leaving a dull, fading afterimage. Most stings feel like a thumbtack prick or the jab of a needle delivering a vaccine. Short, hot, sharp: unwanted but not unbearable.

The visceral response to the sudden sharpness is a rippleshiver of nerve alarm, hairs standing on end. Pain is the body sounding a shrill alarm.

Pain triggers the fight-or-flight response: pupils dilate, heart rate spikes, adrenaline rushes, breath quickens. This is the ancient survival tactic: to fight or get away from that which injures to stay alive.

It is easy to mistake these physiological symptoms for fear. Fear is an emotion. The fear of being injured is instinctual, necessary for survival. Recognizing which injuries are tolerable and which are crucial to avoid requires calm, insightful thought.

Emotions are lightningquick—logical thinking follows after, delayed, the rumble of thunder.

We can react to our emotions and allow them to control our actions. Or we can pause, breathe, wait for the thunder.

I AM STANDING at the edge of my garden, staring off into the distance, one hand tightly wrapped around a clump of my skirt at my hip while pondering what to do about the stinging creature that may or may not be trapped in the waistband of my underwear. Is this badass. Is this dignified.

B is not home, but I am not completely isolated. Beyond my garden, beyond the yard, beyond the reach of my voice is a neighbor's house. If I spotted him and waved, would he see it as a call for help and come over, or would he simply wave back? Is he even home? If he is not, how long should I wait, staring in that direction? What help could I even ask him to give?

Between his house and ours is a road. On this road there are sometimes cars, with people in them. Sometimes, people walk by, with dogs or without, turning their heads to ponder our beehives and odd yard sculpture. What could they do for me, if anything?

EVEN WITHIN THE experience of being stung, there are variations.

A shallow sting on the back of the hand that barely breaks the skin may feel like a quick, hot pinprick and may hardly even swell, may be gone by nightfall. A deep sting administering a thorough dose of venom to the soft flesh of the inner arm may have a lingering, dull ache for several minutes, swell within the hour, and continue to swell across much of the forearm the following day. A firm sting to the forehead will at first manifest as a contained lump, but within a day, the fluid may slip down with gravity and pool around an eye socket, resulting in a face that resembles that of a post-match championship boxer.

In beekeeping communities, a photograph of a facial sting is a badge of honor, and beekeepers know the appearance is far more alarming than the injury. But for the general public, the facial sting might spark concerned queries about apparent assault and battery, requiring the injured person to figure out appropriate ways to disguise or isolate themselves for a few days.

I have tested most of the common homegrown methods for treating a bee sting. Put a very hot compress or hot water on it for a half hour to break down the proteins of the venom. Bandage a freshly sliced piece of onion on the sting site to draw out the toxin. Take an antihistamine to minimize the body's inflammatory response. Apply baking soda, honey, toothpaste, aloe vera, aspirin paste, witch hazel, or vinegar. Apply a poultice of chewed tobacco or plantain leaves. Apply essential oils, meat tenderizer, or activated charcoal. Apply ice. Depending on the immediacy of application and location of the sting, these methods vary from surprisingly effective to useless and messy.

THE EXPERIENCE OF a bee sting is never pleasant, but compared to the pain and trauma of other common injuries such as a broken arm, a sprained ankle, or a deep sunburn, it is relatively low in both pain and inconvenience.

Yet many people are terrified of being stung. They react to the presence of a bee as though it were a gun or syringe of deadly poison. When queried, they cite a childhood experience that left them traumatized and terrified.

Small children are resilient creatures. They are clumsy and awkward, learning their limbs, and tend to fall over and bang their bones, scrape themselves bloody raw, mishandle heavy and sharp objects, and acquire assorted bruises. The tables, floors, and sharp-bladed scissors do not become feared objects. But bees often become creatures to be feared.

When experiencing something new, children react directly to the sensations they experience, but they also look to the adults around them. A child that falls down and does not feel pain will make eye contact with an adult to see if the adult is laughing with joy or wide-eyed with fear, and the child will mirror the adult's response.

The urge to protect can be very strong in an adult that loves and cares for their offspring. Life-threatening bee venom reactions are relatively rare, but the fear of them can be intense. If an adult responds to someone being touched or stung by a bee with high-energy fear and panic, they are not necessarily reacting to the actual incident but rather to the possibilities of what *could* happen. A young child does not know this. If the adult acts upset and afraid, the child also panics, and because they do not understand why the adult is reacting so passionately, the child becomes confused and terrified. And this is what the child remembers: being stung by a bee—whether they had an allergic reaction or not—is intensely upsetting and frightening. A person may remember a childhood incident of intense fear and panic well into adulthood, long after the tangible details of the incident have faded. As adults, they remember what they were taught: bees are scary, and bee stings are dangerous.

MOST WILD ANIMALS have the capacity to inflict harm on another, but they will generally only do so for one of two reasons: to eat or to defend. Both motivations are linked directly to survival. Even a seemingly harmless vegetarian animal such as a rabbit will strike out and draw blood if cornered and attacked.

Honey bees are not predators; they have no need to attack another animal. Yet if they believe they, their queen, or their colony is under attack, they will defend to the death. A honey bee is poorly armed: it stings once, then dies. It is not inclined to sting for frivolous reasons.

If you are not perceived as a threat to a bee or their colony, they will not try to sting you. If you are sitting outside and a bee circles around you several times, they are not sizing you up like a boxer to decide where best to attack you; they are inspecting you to decide if you are something from which they can gather pollen and nectar. If they land on you and stay, they are not threatening you; they see you as a safe place to rest for a moment. If you wave your arms around frantically, they may think you are trying to attack them, or they may get tangled in your clothing and react defensively by stinging, much as a dog or cat may lash out with teeth and claws if their tail is stepped on. But if you stay calm, move and breathe normally, and ensure the bee does not get pinched or tangled in your limbs or clothing, they have no reason to sacrifice their life by stinging you.

With all the hives in our yard, it is impossible for me to work in my garden without encountering them. They buzz among the blooming plants and drink mineral-rich water from the puddles formed by my watering hose. I am mindful of where I put my hands and knees so I don't hurt any bees and potentially get stung, but otherwise I ignore them. They are working, and they are not easily distracted from their tasks, even when I pat their furry backs with a gentle finger.

A bee sting is a small and accidental tragedy. A barefoot walk across the lawn, a hand rested against a flat surface—these small movements can entrap a bee body and cause it to fight back violently. The bee falters and falls to its death, its organic weapon torn from its body.

I AM STANDING in the garden, one fist clenching a wad of fabric that includes part of my skirt, part of my underwear, and a hypothetical insect. I could lean over and pull everything I am holding off and run for the house—but I would be left half-naked in full view of the road and the neighbors. Bee-keeping may be perceived as badass, but I do not wish to give visual confirmation.

I could wait until B gets home or until someone I recognize walks by and call them over to help me. But what could they do? And I might just get stung anyway during the execution of whatever plan we came up with.

A man appears, walking a large dog on a leash along the roadside. He is close enough to call out to. I stare at him, considering. I do not recognize him. He is younger than me, handsome, in classy clothes. Is this someone I would be okay with seeing me half-naked in an awkward situation? What is the polite way to ask someone to help you tear off your clothes and watch you run away?

He turns his head and sees a woman in casual summer clothes, one fist on her hip, looking over the lush greenery of her garden. He waves in pleasant greeting. I wave back with my free hand and smile. Everything is fine here.

I wait until the passerby is out of sight, then slowly, moving only my feet half an inch at a time, turn until I am facing the house. As long as I keep my thighs together, my logic goes, the most tender parts of my anatomy are as protected as they can be. I lean to one side, lifting my foot and wriggling my toes until my loose summer shoe slips off. My plan will not work with floppy footwear creating a tripping hazard.

Squeezing my knees and ankles together, I rise onto my toes and try to walk by moving only my feet. Each step is only a few inches, and I have only one outstretched arm to balance with—broader movements would greatly increase my chance of pinching and angering the hypothetical wasp in my skirt. I move frustratingly slowly through the garden and across the yard, each mincing step a cognitive cacophony of wasp-hiding skirt brushing against my legs and my bare toes crushing leaves and grass that might hide foraging bees.

A car drives by. It sounds alarmingly loud and fast in contrast to my Zen-like focus on bending one foot, then the other, while keeping my knees and ankles together.

I cross the yard. My ankles and the arches of my feet burn with a hot ache. The porch—why is the porch so many inches up, so high off the ground!? Shuffling my feet parallel to the porch edge, I squeeze my knees tighter together and take the risk of awkwardly lifting one foot onto the porch, then tilt my body over it and lift my other foot. No sting.

But now the hypothetical wasp could be between my shins; I should keep them from brushing against each other while I keep my thighs together. I walk across the porch from the knees down, toes pointed inward like a drunken duck, larger steps than before but still so slow.

At the back door of the house I pause, breathe. A realization pops into my head, and I gasp—then I reach out and test the doorknob. It turns, unlocked. I sigh in relief.

I glance toward the only other house visible from where I stand. A neighbor is on his porch, talking to someone, facing me. Perhaps he is on the phone. If I stand motionless and staring at him on my porch for too long, he might wonder what I am doing and call out a conversational greeting to me. I am busy right now and do not have time for chitchat with the neighbor. If he lingers too long, I may have to pretend I am talking on my cellphone. He turns, disappears, and I hear his door click shut.

I hook my free hand into the waistband of my skirt, carefully wiggling my thumb into the elastic of my underwear. I take a deep breath. I have been lucky so far, but this could go very wrong.

Using both hands in one quick movement, I pull my skirt and underwear down and off, dropping them around my feet as I shoulder check the door open, jump indoors, and slam the door behind me.

Inside: me, nervously sweating and half-garbed, gratefully free of any stinging critters, with only a swelling welt on my left hip to show for my quiet misadventure.

Outside, on the porch: a crumpled pile of cotton skirt and underwear, abandoned haphazardly and left to bewilder any unsuspecting delivery person or solicitor.

Beekeeping is badass.

Diner

CLARENCE DOESN'T FARE well in poor weather. He tends to faint when the wind picks up.

On a bright summer afternoon, a Cooper's hawk lands in a tree near the quail pen. He watches the quails for a few minutes, like a hungry patron in a fast-food restaurant pondering the menu board before approaching and placing an order, then swoops down and lands on the ground. He disappears behind the far wall of the pen, and I expect to see him fly off—but after a minute, he comes walking around the side of the pen, cocking his head and looking the wire-and-wood walls up and down, as though in search of a door he can use. He rounds the front of the pen, stepping awkwardly through the long grass, and again disappears behind the back. When he completes the circle and arrives again at the front of the pen, he pauses, turns around, and circles the pen in the opposite direction, stretching and bending his neck, looking for something he is certain is around here somewhere.

After two or three more circles, he stops, ruffles his wings indignantly, stretches his neck to its full length, then again reverses direction, this time faster.

He is almost stomping his feet now; he has traversed this same path so many times that the bent grass is beginning to form a visible trail. He looks altogether like a frustrated restaurant patron circling the building, trying to find an open door. He can see the food inside, soft bodies huddled down with bright, unblinking eyes—if only he could find the way in.

Eventually, I get tired of watching his annoyed drama spook my little birds. I jog toward the pen, waving my arms and yelling something nonsensical; he flies off to a tree. I throw gravel from the driveway at him until he flies off out of sight.

But he will return. And I won't always be there to shoo him away.

I tell B about this little adventure. He disappears into his woodshop, designing and building a simple stick figure mannequin with articulated limbs and an upturned bucket for a head.

I dress Clarence in the finest of scarecrow fashion: an old pair of blue jeans, a long-sleeved shirt, a baseball cap. I stuff wads of shopping bags in his sleeves to form lumpy muscles. On impulse, I glue a large pair of plastic googly eyes to the front of his bucket face.

Stationed at the front corner of the quail pen, Clarence takes to his job well. He can often be found with one knee bent, rectangular foot jauntily resting against the edge of the pen, a fingerless hand nonchalantly flopped on the pen roof. The quails, crows, and rabbits pay him no mind, but the hawk no longer harasses my poultry. A neighbor mentions our quails' security guard is creepy, his wide white eyes staring at her through the darkness when she comes up the driveway at night.

Every strong soul has their weakness, however. Clarence doesn't do well in windstorms. In the morning, I often find him lying down on the job, unblinking eyes staring at the sky, half-buried in wet leaves.

"Everyone needs a rest sometimes," I say as I prop him back up, straighten his cap, squish his muscles back into place. Even a protector of small and soft things sometimes falls down and needs someone to pick him up.

PART 3

Autumn

DURING HARVEST SEASON, certain wild animals are more likely to be encountered in human-inhabited spaces, like orchards and roadways, following the scent of food. Technically, it's not illegal to harvest roadkill in most of Canada. There are certain procedures you should follow, like make sure it's bodywarm and fresh not oldcold and stiff and *Steve help me load this thing n cover it with the tarp while the girls keep an eye out for cars damn it turn that flashlight off fer Chrissakes Shelia if the smell bothers you roll the winder down errybody just act cool if the cops roll by Dave your dad best got that table clear in the g'rage cause we gon be havin us some barbecue next weekend I tell ya!*

Bill

"The other apple tree has to come down," B says.

The first apple tree, the one closest to the house, has an annual crop of blotchy, uneven apples. They are small and mottled with bug spots, too sour to eat fresh but perfect for applesauce and, though dimpled and difficult to peel, fine for pies.

But the other apple tree is barren. It has not produced apples in decades or, depending on who remembers, ever. Its off-kilter branches splay at odd angles; they droop and break when loaded with snow or ice, and B grumbles while clearing the yard of its fallen branches that could snag and break his lawnmower blades. Even the wildlife seems to avoid it—squirrels don't scurry up its trunk, and the birds that build nests in the other trees and in the rafters of the garage give it a wide berth. The tree's trunk is thick with soft, damp, greengray moss and feathery-white lichen.

"It's probably diseased," B says. "It has to come down."

What use is an apple tree that bears no fruit and scatters broken branches across the lawn. Why do the work to clean up after a plant that is ugly and pointless. Why keep an apple tree if not for apples.

B stands at the window and watches as apples on the first tree loosen from their stems and tumblethump to the ground. In the springtime, when the branches are dry and bare of both leaves and snow, he will take a chainsaw to the other tree and be done with it.

⸻

AN ORCHARD WITHOUT bugs produces no fruit.

Native pollinators—wasps, butterflies, bumblebees, mason bees, thousands of species of tiny solitary bees—flit from flower to flower in search of nectar. As they scramble through the petals, their limbs and bodies are inadvertently dusted with pollen. From one flower to the next, the pollen is taken, and thus pollination is done. The flowers, now fertilized by the sharing of pollen, wither and fade as their peduncles swell and grow into fruit, seed.

The skeptics say native pollinators are enough. Sow the seeds, forget the bees, and be done with it.

A single native butterfly is a more efficient pollinator than a single imported honey bee. An acre of organic land can host thousands or tens of thousands of native pollinators. But an acre of land can host *millions* of honey bees.

A crop left to the care of native pollinators will produce some fruit and vegetables . . . *some*. A crop pollinated by colonies of honey bees will grow triple that amount of produce. Native pollinators are efficient, but their numbers are small.

Honey bees, however, are legion.

⸻

IN THE SPRING, the migrating birds return and flutter noisily from tree to tree, scavenging for bugs, calling for mates, and scouting possible nesting sites. I take a brush to our shedding indoor cat and collect soft, clean fistfuls of her fur to set outside. I watch amusedly as the sparrows and robins gather beakfuls of it from a bowl on the porch—the softest souvenir of danger to line their tender nests.

B goes to his workshop to oil the chainsaw and ready it for cutting down the barren apple tree, and I remove the hummingbird feeder from the tree. As I untangle the feeder from the gnarled, twisted branch, I glance up to where the tree's trunk splits in a narrow *y* and see a recognizable clump of twigs and leaves. A small pile, carefully woven, tucked between mossy limbs.

The young of animals are sacred. As a species, we coo and fawn over small things, miniature versions of their adult parents. Even baby predators are seen as something to be patted, held, cared for. Someone is building a home for their offspring in this twisted and rotting tree.

B puts his chainsaw away. I move the hummingbird feeder to another tree to give the future family some quiet privacy. And we wait.

HONEY BEES ARE legion.

And so, too, are humans: legion, many.

In the countryside, people spread out with their farms and gardens and orchards and ranches. In the city, they are densely packed, often hundreds per acre, stacked high in apartment buildings and condominiums.

To stay well-fed and nourished, the average person needs to eat around five hundred pounds of food per year, at least a third of which should be fruits and vegetables. But the tightly packed housing of urban cities allows for little or no growing of food. Every acre of agricultural land must produce enough food to sustain a myriad of people.

If the farmers fail to grow enough food to feed the urban population, the country must import produce from other countries at increased cost and potentially questionable quality and availability. Otherwise, they risk a population that deteriorates into malnutrition: health issues, shortened lifespans, increased burdens on the health care system.

The pressure on farmers to feed the population is immense. They are paid little and are subject to factors they cannot control: blighted crops, misfortunes and accidents, the whims and shifting patterns of weather and climate. There are no good decades, only good years, and of those, rarely two in a row. In the warm seasons, the farmers work; in the cold, they wait, plan, prepare, and hope for better outcomes.

For them to rely entirely on native pollinators to produce—at best—modestly sized harvests would be foolish. They need huge armies of bugs to pollinate their crops to produce enough food. And so, they turn to the large-scale beekeepers of the pollination industry.

OVER THE NEXT few days, a fat, red-breasted robin diligently gathers slim twigs, bits of strings, and dried grass for her nest. And one day, I see her sitting tidily on her completed nest, beak poking over the edge, watching me cautiously.

While she's momentarily away from her home, I set up one of B's tall ladders under the tree, carefully weaving its rungs between the many branches. I climb to its top—but the nest is still above my head. I stretch my arm up and out, phone in hand, and blindly take a quick series of photos, then rush back down the ladder. The robin returns to her nest as soon as my foot touches the ground. She settles in and watches as I review my photos.

Momma Robin has laid three beautiful blue eggs, so perfect and small I could cup them all in my palm at once.

I return to the nest daily. Momma watches me until I start to climb the ladder, then flies from her nest and lands, loudly scolding, on a higher branch while I awkwardly photodocument her home. Within a week, she barely scolds me during my brief visits and lands back on her nest as soon as I take the first rattling, clanking step back down the aluminum ladder.

Every day, the eggs are in a different position—rolled or rotated, from one end of the nest to the other. Momma is working hard to turn her eggs so her babies develop evenly. An unturned egg results in a chick that is deformed, with spine bent or wings twisted, a tiny version of someone who has slept too long in an awkward position. I doubt Momma knows this, but she has some innate urge or is responding to some signal from within the eggs that tells her she must turn them.

I have watched nests before and thus have a reasonably low expectation for this one's future. With the exception of the noisy, invasive starlings who seem to be experts at producing families of obnoxiously shrieking offspring, many inhabited nests end up childless. Predators—rats, hawks, or crows—devour the eggs, or the nest is poorly built or destroyed in a storm. Or the eggs are unfertilized or fail to develop and, after a few weeks, are kicked out of the nest, abandoned, left to rot.

But one afternoon, my photos show a new development. Two of Momma Robin's offspring have hatched out and resemble something the cat had coughed up or bits of raw chicken skin that had fallen behind a linty clothes dryer. The third egg remains unhatched—but this is not unusual. Sometimes, one takes longer to develop and hatches later. I name the two homely children Christopher and Batmanand.

THERE ARE BEEKEEPERS who keep a few hives in their yard or in a field. Perhaps a dozen colonies of bees, though often less, sometimes more.

But most domestic hives in the developed world are owned by pollinator beekeepers. Pollination businesses manage hundreds or thousands of hives they rent out to farmers for the purpose of pollinating crops. A truckload of hives is placed in an orchard while the fruit trees bloom so the honey bees can fertilize the flowers by distributing pollen as they gather nectar for their own food. After a few weeks, when the flowers fade, the hives are moved to another orchard or farm to catch the next crop as it blooms. And another, and another—boosting crop yields one field at a time to feed the legions of people.

EVERY DAY, I photograph the nest, documenting the babies as they sprout feathers and grow into recognizable birds. These are not beautiful photos: they are off-centered and unfocused. Perhaps I do this to remind myself. Perhaps to prove that it happened. In the early days, Christopher and Batmanand are tiny and grotesque with their globular eyes sealed shut. As I approach, their gummy-lipped beaks gape open, and their weak bodies flop and tremble, mistaking me for a parent bringing food. Once their eyes open, they squeeze down into their nest and stare at me, pretending to be invisible.

After a week and a half, Christopher and Batmanand bulge out of the nest, their fat, fully feathered torsos barely fitting. I imagine them to be as soft and weightless as the dead birds I've held, but warm. I want to touch them—but I can't and shouldn't.

As I raise my hand over the nest on the fourteenth day: a sudden flurry of wings. I close my eyes; feathers and leaves smack my face, and the birds are—gone. Fledged. My photos show only a blur of brown and green, motion.

Left alone in the nest is poor Eggbert the Unhatched, abandoned and rotting, surprisingly uncracked. Momma does not return, and after a few days, Eggbert is also gone, scavenged by squirrels or rats or crows.

I look up through the branches, through the leaves at the egg-blue sky, and wonder what the yard will look like once this tree is gone. Why would we keep an apple tree that produces no apples. The topmost leaves flutter and turn on their stems, hundreds of hands waving goodbye.

And between the fluttering, softly flapping leaves: a small, unfluttering green thing. An apple.

———

A HEALTHY HONEY bee colony can bring in far more nectar than it needs, and the extra is stored as honey. Between moving hives, the pollination beekeepers extract this honey from their hives. But they are far too busy with hauling hives to do much with the honey other than extract it. They make their money from fertilizing flowers in farmers' fields, not from wrangling retail contracts and designing advertising campaigns. The pollination beekeepers bulk sell the honey in big metal barrels to distributors for pennies per pound.

The distributors package the honey in jars, bottles, and buckets, label it with a brand they have designed, named, and promoted, and place it on retail store shelves. The retail price of the honey is not based on the original beekeepers' production cost of the honey but on the distributors' expenses ... and on whatever number the end consumer is willing to pay.

The price of the honey is far below the cost of production.

PERHAPS IT WAS a shift in the climate that caused this tree to produce a flower, bloom, and develop a fruit. Perhaps it was the mild pruning I'd accidentally given the tree the previous fall, absentmindedly, before realizing I was working on the wrong tree. Perhaps it was the decades-old compost bin by its roots that I'd excavated to harvest fertilizer for my garden, resulting in an unkempt mess of worm-rich, ancient compost being inadvertently strewn across its roots. Perhaps it was something to do with our beehives.

We dismiss all these possibilities in favor of the fantastically obvious: the tree had overheard us discussing cutting it down due to its lack of productivity, so it produced a single apple, a Hail Mary held proudly against the sky.

We agree that the tree will not be cut down until the apple falls.

No other apples are on that tree—just the one, lonely and proud against the sky. The first tree has its usual extravagant crop of dimpled, spotty apples.

Come autumn, I listen for the *ba-dump-bump* of ripe apples hitting the ground beneath the first apple tree. I gather up a ladder and some buckets and collect them, plucking them from their branches and scooping them from the ground. The ones that are rotting or full of wormholes go into the compost bin. The bruised ones are left in a pile by the trail, where the silent-footed deer cross our property at night. The best ones are brought inside to chop into pies and simmer into applesauce. The rest are piled in layers between sheets of newspaper and stacked in a storage shed to be put out for the deer and rabbits when the winter turns February gray and food sources are scarce.

But the apple atop the other tree does not fall.

Most fruits—apples, tomatoes, berries—grow to ripeness, then either split open or fall from their plant. That's how their seeds end up on the ground, where they can take root and grow into new plants. But this apple is stubborn. It doesn't behave like all the other apples. It isn't just gonna go along with the rest of the orchard.

We name the apple Bill. It seems an appropriate name for a stubborn curmudgeon resistant to change.

Leaves fall, the autumn rains come, and through it all, Bill stays put, a dark spot against a pewter sky, surrounded by bare branches. Hungry squirrels scavenge the last few rotting apples caught in the topmost branches of the first tree, but they do not touch Bill.

I give the first tree its annual mid-winter pruning, thinning the branches and removing excess growth. I do not bother to prune the other tree. There is no point in caring for a tree that will soon be felled.

Come spring, I toss the last of the now-withered winter apples by the trail for the deer then scrub and refill the bird feeders. The trees' new leaves unfurl; the returning migratory hummingbirds flit and buzz among the feeders. The first apple tree bursts into a fragrant white halo of blossoms. And above it all, Bill the apple hangs stubbornly—a little darker, a little wrinkled, but still hanging on.

And beneath him, a few branches down, a small, surprising cluster of apple blossoms.

Spring warmth turns into a summer heat wave, the longest in a decade. Plants fade and wither, the grass turns to stiff brown straw, dust billows from our feet when we walk across the lawn.

After four months of no rain, the drought breaks into an incredible windstorm. The ground is so dry that trees' roots lift from the soil like spoons from sugar bowls, sending huge pines and firs crashing across roads and onto buildings. The sky rains thick with pine needles and dry leaves ripped from dying plants. Power lines whip and snap like electric gunshots, leaving hundreds of thousands of households without power for days.

Then, the rains come. Sweet, rich rain turning the dusty soil into streams of mud and replenishing the parched water table beneath our well.

When the skies calm, we emerge to clean up the yard and check on our neighbors. The ground beneath the first apple tree is littered with half-grown green apples, but there are still enough on the tree to predict a decent autumn harvest. As we clear the fallen branches and debris from the yard, I keep an eye out for Bill. He should be on the ground somewhere, but who knows where after all that wind.

I don't find him there.

I look up, and there, on the topmost branch that hadn't been broken by the wind, is Bill.

BACKYARD BEEKEEPERS, WITH our handfuls of hives and our homemade jar labels, do not have the massive overhead costs of employees and large-scale distribution—but neither do we have the benefits of corporate contracts with chain stores and supermarkets. We have a few precious bee colonies, our own hands, countless hours of heavy labor, and a table at the farmers' market.

If we were to calculate all our expenses—bees, equipment, protective gear, tools, medications, replacement colonies for those that are lost, extraction equipment, jars, all the hours of work at even minimum wage—and divide it by the volume of honey for sale, the price tag would be triple or quadruple that of honey sold in retail stores. The consumers would turn their backs. The honey would be abandoned, unsold.

We price our jars with a number the market will bear: slightly higher than the average retail but low enough that it will still sell. In a good year, we will break even on recouping our costs. A bad year will never be recovered.

The price of the honey is below the cost of production.

AS AUTUMN PROGRESSES, I wait for the *ba-dump-bump* sound of fruit hitting the ground, then harvest all the apples from the first tree. I can't reach the few apples growing beneath Bill, so I wait for them to fall on their own, then add them to the boxes of apples to be saved for the winter deer. Through it all, Bill just hangs there, though now he is so black and wrinkled he looks more like a burl on a diseased twig than anything resembling an apple.

The winter rains come. The bird nests in the rafters of the garage fall to ruin, crumbling down like abandoned barns. I fill the hummingbird feeders with thicker nectar that withstands freezing, toss a few wrinkled apples by the deer trail, pluck the last of the cat fur from the elbows of the now-leafless first apple tree.

One morning in November, I glance up and Bill is—gone. After a year and a half of tenaciously holding on, through two full seasons of blossoms, fruit, and harvest, Bill has finally let go.

I search for him beneath his tree, kicking at the layers of leaves with my feet, and eventually find him. He looks like a small piece of blackened driftwood, feels like a flap of mistreated leather that had accidentally been soaked and cooked in a load of laundry wash. He is so light and fragile. Only his woody little stem, still thick and sturdy, identifies him as an actual fruit.

We name the tree he came from Bill, in memory of the apple of unusual longevity.

BEES FLY FIFTY thousand miles and visit two million flowers to make a pound of honey. Each teaspoon of honey is the life's work of a half-dozen bees. The flavors vary subtly with the varieties and quantities of flowers: each mouthful is as unique as a palmful of snowflakes. There is no value to this that can be translated, no currency exchange rate that recognizes this. These are precious drops that can only be appreciated by consuming them.

I save one jar from each honey harvest, label it, and tuck it away on our shelf of archives. There is no benefit to this, no investment, no end goal. There is only the amazement of tasting one year against the next and comparing. *Here is the summer of the windstorms. This is the year the wasps took out five hives.* Or, *That was when the bulldozers came.*

One day, when we are gone, these will all be eaten, stirred into tea or spread on toast, the stories of each harvest lost and forgotten. And they will wonder why this jar is dark like molasses, why that one is pale golden and sweet. And they will wonder and enjoy. And then it will be gone.

I CUP THE tiny, ancient, withered lump that was once an apple protectively in my hand and find a small glass box to put him in. I add him to my shelf of other curios and small souvenirs.

The skull of a rat I unearthed in the garden. A tiny and perfect paper wasps' nest. Raw quartz crystals from the lake I swam in as a child. A stick gifted by a crow. Skulls and bones and teeth. These small and fragile mementos have no worth, no financial value. They are not milestone markers of significant achievements. They are props for stories. I hang my memories on them.

When I am gone, they will be thrown out, their histories

forgotten. Or they will be saved and carried about for years until they rattle into dust, dry decomposition.

———

WHY KEEP BEES if not for honey, for money.

Why do anything, really, that doesn't make money.

Why collect rocks from the seashore, paint figurines of dancing pigs, or build models of tiny cars. Why learn to dance, practice weaving colorful bits of thread, or take lessons in archery. Why play a sport if not for paid competitions. Why sing. Why stack bits of wood into something not useful. Why keep pets.

Why keep animals if not for necessary food or protection or service. Why keep anything that costs more than it profits you. A pretty light that increases the electricity bill. A vintage car that needs extra insurance. Why, really.

Why prune and trim the apple trees for apples you won't eat. Why be proud of an accomplishment that gets thrown away or left for waste. Why learn about anything you'll never put to use. Why be curious. Why build a fire only to burn it.

Why do anything.

———

NOW, THE FIRST tree produces its annual crop of small, mottled apples, too tart to eat but perfect for baking and applesauce.

And Bill the tree grows more and more apples each year, scattered among the leaves like big green jewels.

I harvest all the apples from the first tree. But I don't pick the apples that hang from Bill.

One fall morning nearly three years after I noticed that first stubborn apple, I hear the familiar tumble and thump of an apple hitting the ground. I hurry out into the yard and retrieve it from beneath Bill before the squirrels or deer can get it. I bring it into the house, wash it, and cut a slice. It is rich and sweet, with delicate flavor.

I have heard tell that your heart is the size of your fist. I curl my hand into a fist, hold it against B's, and compare. Bill's apples are huge, the size of our two fists—or our two hearts—together, and they hang low enough that I can reach them with a short step ladder.

I don't pick them. I wait for them to fall on their own. They are huge and sweet as life itself, and maybe, like Bill the apple before them, they just want to hang out for a while.

Sustenance

I DUMPED OUT THE bunny trough. Now, in autumn, it has become unnecessary, needed only by fungi and breeding bugs.

We were lucky to have been in a position to provide sanctuary, blessed to have water to offer. Throughout the summer drought, we remained untouched by tightening municipal water restrictions: We're on an acreage in an agricultural community with only our own well to draw from. While the lawn baked to a crisp brown dust, the garden stretched into overgrown green lushness, thriving on the incessant heat and the constant slow drip of the soaker hose. A thick green halo of dandelions and grass sprouted around the edges of the garden boxes, a startling contrast from the barren, brown dryness of the rest of the property.

In an attempt to ease the dehydration death rate of wild birds by maintaining makeshift bird baths during the drought, I'd drooped a loop of the soaker hose over one edge of a garden box and sunk a plastic tub in the ground to catch the drips. Mindful of the baby rabbits that lived under the shed and in the forest beside us, B put a cement brick in the tub so any little ones that fell in could get a foothold to climb out.

The rainless days had turned to weeks, then months. Dust billowed from our steps when we walked. The air was bright and harsh, unforgiving.

But every day that I visited the garden, I'd startle a rabbit or two grazing in the oasis of green weeds around the garden boxes. Or I'd see a long-legged deer and her tiny, rubber-nosed fawn as they trotted off into the trees. The ever-moist soaker hoses were always coated in thirsty bees from our hives. And in the evening, if I walked quietly, I would see families of rabbits having their dinner or napping in the lengthening tree shadows. They'd become accustomed to me: They'd bolt if startled but would otherwise give me a wide berth, watching from a side-eye as I noodled about in the garden.

We suspected that once the heat faded at night, while we slept behind walls not ten feet from the garden, there was more unseen activity outside. In the morning, I'd dump out the bunny tub to kill any mosquito larvae and set it back into its hole to be slowly refilled. Despite the lack of wind, I'd always find the tub water dirty with bits of grass and twigs—it reminded me of backwash crumbs in a dog's water bowl. The occasional beet in my garden would have bare, leafless stems, as though it had been tidily trimmed with scissors. The youngest tips of the tomato plants looked lopped off by shears. In the dry dirt, the occasional clue: the heart-shaped dent of a deer hoofprint.

Friends suggested I build a fence or put netting over the plants. I declined: I could buy beets and tomatoes at the store, but there was no such resource or currency for the wildlife. I could afford to spare a few samples.

The rain has returned, and with it, autumn. The lawn now sprouts green. I pull up the bunny trough, scrape the algae from its bottom, turn off the soaker hoses. The rabbits, once plentiful, are now but a few, lost to natural selection and the rural neighborhood road. Even the coyotes do not yodel and *kai-whoop* in the fields as often as they did a few months ago.

We have too many beets, and the tomatoes, though yet green, are plentiful. I cut the heads from our sunflowers and brush their hundreds of seeds into containers to scatter for the birds. Remembering the squirrel I'd watched last winter steal a lone gray-rotten apple from one of our trees, I ponder where to store all the apples I've gathered. Winter is coming, and the deer will return, with the squirrels and the rabbits and the chickadees.

A Throne for Your Heaven

ONE PERSON'S JUNK is another's treasure. One person's hell is another's heaven. Who am I to judge?

Our neighbor Josie keeps chickens on her porch. Not in cages or pens, just on the porch like house cats, roosting in the deck chairs and pecking at the spots on the sliding glass door. The chicken run is the front yard, outlined in a flimsy, handmade fence that blows over in a stiff wind. Every so often while washing dishes at the kitchen sink, I'll glance out the window and holler "Chicken!" and B will sneak out the door and try to catch whatever wayward bird has wandered into our yard.

The chickens have no nesting boxes, and we never see Josie gathering the eggs they lay randomly in her yard. And the chickens are far too old to be slaughtered for meat. We're not sure why Josie keeps chickens, but she doesn't like us, so we've never asked.

Instead of a water trough and shed in the chicken run, Josie has a trampoline and an upholstered brown armchair. The trampoline catches rainwater and provides shade, but we're not sure about the armchair. We theorize that perhaps Josie intends to sit there with a cup of tea and a good book, spending time with her feathered friends, but we never see her sitting in the chair. In fact, we rarely see her, except when the fence blows down and she runs around the neighborhood trying to round up her wandering chickens.

One morning over breakfast, B gestures through the window at the sky and comments, "So that's why she's keeping chickens."

I look up to see a chicken. In the sky. On either side of the bird: huge, flapping wings. Domestic chickens don't really fly.

"So that's why she's keeping chickens," B repeats. "To feed the eagles."

ONCE UPON A time, the house that Josie lives in was occupied by a young couple. The swept-clean driveway was shaded by a double row of well-pruned trees, and hanging flowers spilled from potted plants on the porch. She baked bread and pastries, and he mowed the lawn on Saturdays.

Now, the trees are gone, replaced by thick, rotting stumps. The roof of the house is shoddily patched, and it likely leaks. The yard decor includes a pile of broken furniture and garbage bags, a cloudy-windowed car blanketed in leaves and pine needles, and a toilet. The lawn is long and full of seedy weeds. The windows of the house never open.

ONCE UPON A time, the metropolis to our west was small and surrounded by even smaller towns. Its center grew tall, densely packed with high-rise apartment buildings and office towers, and its outskirts spread, puddle-like, engulfing the closer settlements.

A rock dropped in water in slow motion will first break the surface, then produce a sharp splash upward where it landed, then an ever-expanding circle of outward-moving waves. The growth of the metropolis' center creates first a displacement of those within its midst, then a rippleshift of renovation and relocation that upheaves first the surrounding communities, then the next towns over, then the next.

The people displaced by this urban-industrial progress are moving to the outskirts. Under the pressure of a growing population, the outskirt communities are bulldozing older homes, forests, and farms, building more buildings and more housing for more people. And the former inhabitants of those bulldozed homes are rippling even farther beyond, outward.

When hermit crabs outgrow their shells, they line up on the beach from largest crab to smallest. The biggest crab finds a new shell and moves into it. The next crab moves into the newly vacated shell. Then the next and the next, down the line until the final shell is abandoned and left to be adopted by a wanderer or demolished by the waves.

In this rapidly growing city, people also rearrange themselves and trade their housing, though not so tidily. Landowners pocket the payments from the sales of their properties and purchase prettier homes elsewhere. Renters flutter about frantically like wind-scattered leaves and likewise land on the outskirts, often in older or less-valued homes—or if they resist leaving their locale, they downsize into smaller units, trading houses for apartments. The denser the population, the smaller the home each human can call their own.

Urban progress imposes a grid on the landscape that continually grows finer, tighter. The arbitrary lines cut the land smaller, never larger. Acreages and single-house lots become rows of condos, duplexes, apartment buildings. But a towering high-rise never becomes a sprawling farm.

The habits and presence of the wild animals are shifting as the surrounding neighborhood is bulldozed and developed from wild habitat and farms into condo complexes and giant, overpriced houses on tiny lots. There are fewer butterflies now, their fields of flowers gone. But there are also fewer mosquitoes, their population a casualty of the local swamp being filled in with gravel and dirt. Our contrasting reactions to these two changes are subjective and focused on our own comfort.

Where once we used to see the occasional misplaced cow or chicken wandering down the road, families of deer jaywalking from one orchard to another, or millions of tiny frogs migrating from their tadpole ponds, now we see coyotes, scavengers. And frequent roadkill: hawks and owls, yearling deer, opossums that instinctively play dead in front of approaching cars. A regal river otter with doglike paws and a tail as thick as my arm is hauled home by B and ceremoniously buried in my garden. So many wild animals have lost their trees, their rivers, their fields to the bulldozers and backhoes and are frantically trying to find new homes. Those that can move to the less-populated outskirts. Those that remain flail about frantically, trying to survive in an ever-tightening grid of roads now packed with cars and the shrinking yards of people who spray pesticides, rip out weeds, and throw stones at small, unwanted trespassers.

The long-legged cranes have left. The forest songbirds have moved into the trees on our and our neighbors' properties or have gone farther east, away from the spreading metropolis, into forests and farmlands. And we, too, will soon need to migrate elsewhere, because our neighborhood—including our little acreage, with Bill the apple tree, the ashes of the beehive we had to euthanize, the otter buried in my garden, the leftover lost toys from the children who were raised here—will be bulldozed in a few years to accommodate the spread of the metropolis. Growth creates displacement, ergo species relocation. We can either stay in situ and become frantic and cramped, or we can move elsewhere and survive.

AS THE MONTHS go by, through spring rain and summer heat, we grow increasingly concerned about Josie's chickens' well-being, but the birds look fat and healthy, and a garden hose appears, snaking its way across Josie's lawn, dripping onto the trampoline. The armchair develops a pale layer of caked dust and chicken excrement.

B and I develop multiple theories about Josie's armchair. Perhaps it has some symbolic meaning or sentimental value to Josie or the chickens. Perhaps it is infested with some kind of flea or bug the birds like to eat. Perhaps it is some kind of installation art piece. *La chaise de l'excrement de poulet.* Materials used: La-Z-Boy reclining chair, chickens, chicken shit, dirt.

One morning over breakfast, we look out the window and notice the chickens are gone, and the makeshift fence has been pulled up and piled in a corner of Josie's yard. Over the next week, we see more of Josie than we have in a year as she and a companion haul out her possessions into a pickup truck and ferry them away. And one morning, the day before the rent is due, the truck is gone, the trampoline is gone, Josie is gone.

IT IS ONLY within language that we attribute a movement downward, or the decay of a physical entity, with negativity.

We associate downward movement with regression, moving backward, and upward movement with forward progress, growth, improvement. But these are only words. Within nature, it is a normal process. Movement forward is not always the building up or enlarging of something; often, it is the breaking down, the disintegration.

A tree falls in the forest. Its branches become a haven for small forest floor animals seeking sanctuary. As its wood dries, it becomes home to beetles and bumblebees that burrow and tunnel. The wood crumbles and falls to the ground, a mulch blanket protecting seeds and insect cocoons. Eventually, it breaks down and becomes dirt, soil for new trees to sprout from.

Decades ago, a beautiful new house on the outskirts of this metropolis was its owners' treasured home. Then, the owners moved on to live elsewhere, perhaps to a larger home to accommodate offspring or to a smaller one after the children had grown and left. The house became a rental unit, inhabited by someone who called it home but did not own it. The house was no longer new, and sometimes, things needed repair; when something broke, the tenants may not have had the permission or ability to do the repairs themselves, and the landlords may have been incentivized to do the bare minimum of work to keep profits high.

After years of renters, the house shows its age. The owners have sold or passed away; the new owners are often investors or real estate developers who are not as invested in the sentimentalities of the house's history. They may view it solely as a source of rental income, a technicality to be maintained as needed until they can resell or develop the property for greater profit. The renters come and go. The claw marks of unruly pets are painted over but still visible. Residual rot from a leaking pipe softens the floorboards.

The door hangs slightly crooked, leaking warmed air. The foundation settles, shifts, and a thin crack spiders up a wall.

Higher-income tenants decline to inhabit the house, its aging carpets and overpainted walls beneath their standards. A more-forgiving echelon of tenants moves in. They are tolerant of pipes that rattle, a ceiling that bows and is stained.

Times change. The house ages. Perhaps it changes owners a few times. The costs to keep the house at a reasonable living standard become too frequent, too high. Another pipe bursts and rots out the flooring and walls. Or vintage wiring causes a fire. The house is boarded up and sits empty, hollow, a fallen tree. Squatters move in.

We could call this ugly or unwelcome, this state of falling into decay. We associate such characteristics with neglect and disuse. But we see only a glimpse, a glance, a few decades' sample of a much grander process. The moral judgments we place on such decomposition and decrepitude are subjective and partial.

"The neighborhood has gone downhill," some say. As though those of lower or no income, or of poorer yard maintenance habits, were not worthy of a home.

The property is sold, subdivided. The house is bulldozed. New homes are built, and multiple driveways are paved where there had been one. Bigger houses with small lawns and huge price tags. And the cycle begins again.

KNOWING THAT IT will likely be months before the absentee landlord takes any action, B and I are concerned about the building next door sitting empty with Josie's abandoned garbage on the porch and an unkempt lawn. There are people who tend to break into things, have parties in abandoned buildings, and set up shop for all manner of illicit businesses. We put on gloves, get garbage bags, clean up the yard, hose down the filth-covered porch. We collect various abandoned objects—flowerpots, gardening tools, a coffee table—and leave them at the end of the driveway where they are randomly repossessed by passersby.

Behind the house, we find the chicken-shit chair. We don't get too close—it exudes an odor of swamp, of rotting septic tank. Grass and moss are sprouting from its creases. Its brown upholstery is mottled with gray and green mildew, with thick white splotches of chicken excrement.

FOR SOME THIRTY years, our family has lived on this acreage, in this neighborhood of small farms and wildlife and rural ideologies. The back end of the property was a belt of trees and brambles. Beyond, the ground dipped down into ninety acres of municipal forest, an abandoned industrial gravel mine overtaken with trees and tangled fields of wild berries and clover; a green-scented swamp fed by a beaver-dammed creek and punctuated with ducks and muskrat-like swimming rodents; eagles, hawks, a stealthy bobcat stalking rabbits; and the quiet nests of deer and coyotes.

Now, all that has been buried beneath months of machines. The forest has been flattened, scraped away, and replaced with mounds of dirt piled without public explanation. Where has the bobcat gone, the beavers? The deer step elegantly down our driveway, my tongueclicks and whistles mere curiosities against the backdrop of banging machinery. This is Progress.

The lawn is riddled with windstorm branches: With the protective forest gone, the wall of trees at the back end of our property is vulnerable to wind, cracks, breakage. Progress.

Flaps of neon surveyor's tape trace a line through the underbrush. Here there be green and home—beyond, The Great Nothing, a wasteland of barren forget. Progress, you look remarkably like erasure, a yawning and empty hunger.

The surveyor tape is loosely knotted around tree branches and is thus easily removed, balled in a stubborn fist, and garbaged. It makes no difference against the straight lines of bureaucratic plans, but—Principles. Defiance. A rabbit scurries from the underbrush, bolting toward our house, garden, weed-riddled lawn. I stand in the tree line, squinting into the dust, facing Progress.

WE KEEP AN eye on the house next door, keep the vandals out, and eventually, a couple moves in. We shake hands over the fence, and they say they got a sweet deal: six months of half-price rent in exchange for fixing up the place. Apparently, Josie had left the inside of the house in even worse shape than the outside.

They're an industrious pair. They put on some good music, open the windows, and start ripping up carpets, repairing walls. Their pickup truck fills with an assortment of broken furniture and garbage for the dump. The end of their driveway is a constantly changing freebie pile of furniture and household objects for neighbors and visitors to pick through.

Eventually, the new neighbors discover the chicken-shit chair. They load it onto a dolly and wheel it to the end of the driveway. B and I are baffled but say nothing. Perhaps they are just storing it there out of the way until the next trip to the dump. Or perhaps there's something special about this chair that we're unaware of. The next day it rains—hard rain, for several days. When the sun returns, the chicken-shit chair sits steaming by the roadside, a little less dusty but still festooned with sprouting grass and clumps of barn-yard refuse.

THE YEAR AFTER the forest that had overtaken the gravel mine was bulldozed, the flavors of our honey changed. Our spring harvest, which in previous years had been a rich orange-gold color and sweetly sour as children's candies, was now lemon yellow, the tart note reduced to a quiet zing at the end of a taste. Our summer honey, once light and mellow, nearly pale as water, darkened and became bolder in flavor. The rich burnt-caramel flavor of our autumn harvest became more subtle, less surprising, though its oxblood color remained the same.

The chemical composition of honey is contingent upon the varieties of flowers the bees forage upon. The flower nectar creates the flavor; the pollen, the color. Alfalfa begets honey that is vibrant and sweet, with a recognizable golden color. Late-summer knotweed and autumn trees produce honey that is as dark and rich as organic chocolate. Fireweed honey tastes like a sunrise and can be so pale a clear glass jar of it appears empty.

Wildflower honey, unlike monocrop honeys from hives that are placed in single-crop fields, is a mélange of all the random wild and domestic flowers that grow in the area. Thus, a mixed honey from hives high in the wild mountains will taste distinctly different from one produced by bees in a coastal valley of farms and fields or from colonies kept in suburban backyards with cultivated flowerbeds and vegetable gardens.

And unlike single-source honey that retains its flavor from year to year, wildflower honey is mutable and unpredictable, sensitive to shifts in weather patterns and changes to the geographical landscape. Most flowers only bloom for a few days or weeks, and the bees do not fly in a strong wind or when it is cold. So, a week of hard rain during the spring fruit tree bloom will result in a wildflower honey that has less apple-blossom nectar content and thus tastes different than a honey produced during a spring of solid sun when all the early blooms, including fruit blossoms, could be accessed. And a hive next to a forest that has been bulldozed and flattened for urban development will create a honey that is different from when the forest and its groves and ponds were full of marsh flowers, dandelions, wild berries, and sour cherry trees.

Every fourth or fifth year is a hard one: too much wind and rain, the winter cold is split by a shock of warmth that throws the natural cycles into chaos, or the summer heat wave is parched and dry, crackling with dust. Every few years, the cottontail rabbits overpopulate and spread disease among themselves and die off. Every few years, the wasps take over, infecting more attics and toolsheds than usual, killing beehives and ruining summer patio parties. Every few years, too many honey bee colonies die of parasites or wasps or disease or poor weather patterns.

When I explain to someone that our honey tastes a bit different this year, that the harvest was exceptionally low, or that most of the bees died because of the spring rains, the summer heat wave, or the fact that the rows of commercial chicken barns down the road surrounded with manure-rich, weed-filled land have been torn down and replaced with a grid of copy-pasted giant houses with tiny manicured lawns, they generally respond with a shake of the head and a sigh. "So sad," they say. "I hope it gets better."

As though any season, any year, were a new day, concise and unaffected by the one before it. As though the weather and the phases of the earth's turnings were hard-edged and distinct. As though the ecology were stable, something that existed in a consistent state of being, unchanging. As though evolution and adaptation only happened in our history and are not processes that are ongoing, continuous.

***

ONE MORNING OVER breakfast, B gestures out the window. A weathered pickup truck is idling by the side of the road in front of Josie's house. Two men with scruffy beards and baseball caps are loading the chicken-shit chair into the back of their truck. They look happy, energized. Apparently, the pile of freebies at the end of the neighbor's driveway had caught their eyes—they'd pulled over, seen the decrepit armchair heavy with rainwater, speckled with grass and chicken dung, and one or both had decided, "Yes! I want this! I have a use for this!" And now, they are loading this fragrant, damp piece of furniture into their vehicle and hauling it off to its new home.

One person's garbage is another's treasure. One person's hell is another's heaven. Who am I to judge?

High Tea
With Royalty

THE BLACK-TAILED BUCK steps silently, elegantly across our lawn, his hooves leaving delicate heart-shaped dents in the muddy earth. He looks toward me, twitches his ears, then snorts and turns away. I am not worth his attention.

I try to count the tines on his magnificent crown of antlers, but the tree branches behind his head confuse and dazzle my eyes.

I keep a respectful distance—deer are nonaggressive, but if cornered or threatened, they will strike out with hooves and antlers. The buck's body is sleek, but his shoulder and haunch muscles are solid and powerful, the product of years of fighting with competitors and defending his does and fawns from predators. Deer cause more human deaths than sharks.

He stops by the apple trees, looks in all directions, his down-filled ears twitching this way and that, checking for danger. He pauses and poses, a photogenic celebrity nonchalantly showing off every handsome angle to the paparazzi.

The buck lifts his head up among the apple tree's branches, sniffs at the apples, then carefully selects one and takes a delicate and precise bite. He chews.

Chunks of apple fall from his face as his jaw slides side to side, mouth open. Spittle flies about and drips. His tongue flaps and licks. The buck is a handsome and ignorant prince, grabbing his fork with fist and sloppily shoveling food into his maw like a messy toddler. I have seen cattle and dogs eat with more grace and dignity. I half expect him to belch loudly.

The buck eats five or six apples, each time showcasing atrocious table manners, then freezes and regally stares off into the darkness, his ears cocked. He takes a few steps toward the fence, then pauses, bobbing his head a bit, judging the height of its top rail.

He swiftly tilts up on his hips, lifting his front legs and folding them to his chest—and with a seemingly effortless thrust of his hind legs, he gracefully vaults over the fence and silently trots off into the night. Behind him, there is only a tangled map of heart-shaped hoofprints, a scattering of wet and browning apple chunks, to mark the passing by of this elegant and rude nobility.

PART 4

Winter

IN THE WINTER, dead bees outside a hive are a sign that a colony is alive.

Bees throw their dead outside to keep the hive clean. It's not as noticeable in the summer, when the ground is grassy; the corpses are more visible in the snow. If there's fresh dead bees outside the hive, that means there's enough live bees inside to do the work of throwing them out. The sight can be a bit shocking to see at first, but it's a sign of a healthy hive functioning well.

Burying the Bones

This essay contains references to the graves of Indigenous children at residential schools. This subject matter may be painful. Some readers may wish to skip ahead to the following chapter.

Today, I am burying another of my quail hens. They don't live very long—a handful of years—so this death, though acceptably sad, is not unexpected.

I wrap the bird in a bit of fabric: an old dish towel, perhaps, or a square torn from a worn and thinning bedsheet. This is not so much ritual or reverence, nor squeamishness and covering the face of the deceased, but practicality. Burying a body is a solid and predictable process—but accidentally unearthing one is discord: awkward, uncomfortable. And most graves are not marked with a cross or stone. I have no reason to bury fabric in the earth save for shrouding the dead. If I dig a hole and see a bit of colored fabric, I stop and put the dirt back to not disturb the dead further.

On days of unreasonable weather—extreme heat, heavy rain, or deep snow and cold—it is difficult to dig a grave, so I set the shrouded bird in a closed plastic bin on the porch to deal with the next day. Or I follow my mother's method of entombing dead pets when the ground is too frozen to dig into: wrapped in layers of plastic and brown paper, tucked into a corner of the household deep freezer until the ground softens with the spring thaw. It is important, when temporarily storing bodies in the freezer, to label them carefully and clearly, lest you forget and mistake Jerry the cat or Suki the budgie for a package of steaks or a rack of lamb and set them on the counter to thaw for dinner.

WE BURY OUR dead to honor them. To hold them close while letting them go.

We bury the dead to return them to the earth. Ashes to ashes, dust to dust, meat to the soil that grows the plants that feed the meat.

We bury the dead to honor, to dishonor, or sometimes to just dispose.

The bones of a fish that is caught and eaten are buried, preferably near its home, with a quiet thanks. This is tradition, religion. The wet and festering remnants of a wild animal killed on the lawn by poison or predator are buried with held breath and a small prayer. This is common sense: to prevent the interest of pests and carrion foragers.

The bodies of our dead are also buried—a practicality that spans continents, predates organized religion. Through millennia of social evolution, we learned that burying the dead prevents them from rising up as ghosts or demons in the form of malicious contagious diseases and scavenging predators that would kill the rest of us. In areas where burial in the earth is impossible or impractical, the bodies of our dead are hoisted up in trees, burned, or released into the ocean. Get the bodies away from us—give them back to nature to keep us alive. And we built our myths around this. Thus, common sense became religious ritual became common practice.

In Western society, we bury our dead with great pomp and circumstance, symbolism and ceremony. Witnesses dressed in traditional colors watch the process. A carved marker pinpoints the location. We place them in an urn, vault, or carved wooden box or wrap them in a shroud at the base of a tree. We say we are letting them go, letting them pass from this world into the next—but we cling to the idea of location. Where is the grave. On whose shelf is the jar of cremains, or where were they scattered. We keep them tied to a place, a specific location and physical state, so we can reassure ourselves that we know where the ghosts are—the ghosts, the diseases, the unseen and unknown that we fear.

Some dead are buried hastily, haphazardly, without thoughtful ritual. We associate this with foul play, as though it were part of a game that all participants consented to be part of. We search for our dead desperately, for decades if need be, so we can unearth them and rebury them in a location and manner of which we approve. Even the anonymous dead that are randomly found are collectively mourned, their stories and families sought until they can be returned home. We need to know where the dead are, who the dead are, to feel safe in our bones.

We dig up the bones of nameless children, return them to their homes, and rebury them. They are so small. There are so many of them.

IN THE 1800S, the Canadian government implemented a plan to systemically eradicate Indigenous culture and identity.

Indigenous children were forcibly taken from their families, isolated from their communities and culture, and placed in church-run, government-funded residential schools to be indoctrinated in Christian beliefs and assimilated into Western society. In addition to being an intense forced-immersion program where children were forbidden from referencing their own culture, speaking their mother tongue, or even using their own names, this pedagogy was a violent and abusive reprogramming of young minds. The National Centre for Truth and Reconciliation reports that school staff commonly inflicted emotional, physical, and sexual abuse on the children. Some of the schools were simply forced-labor camps. Others conducted brutal medical experiments on the children without their parents' knowledge or consent. Little or no contact was permitted between the children and their relatives, often for years on end. Death was common: from violence, from neglect, from starvation, from contagious disease, from post-rape childbirth complications. The babies that were born simply disappeared, undocumented, unacknowledged, as though they had never existed.

The children and their children were buried on-site, often without their families or authorities being informed, and their graves went unmarked. Families' queries were ignored, their questions unanswered.

For over a century and a half, the Canadian government continued to approve of and fund the residential schools. The last one closed in 1996. The bones are still being discovered.

AS I STOMP my shovel into the ground, carving out a tiny grave for my quail, a thin breeze from the far end of the property brushes my back. It smells flat, monochromatic, not at all like the rich and varying bouquet of tree sap and swamp grass I used to breathe.

Once upon a time, the ninety acres behind our property was a gravel mine. Huge holes were dug in the ground and interwoven with dusty roads and piles of uprooted trees. Great trucks loaded up tons of unearthed glacial till for use in construction in the nearby city. Around the mine, a thin band of untouched wildland thick with trees, salal, and the occasional rotting remnants of floor beams from hundred-year-old cabins. Around that, land divided into squares: farms and fields and houses, a tiny corner store, roads.

As the gravel mine fell into disuse and the gates around it rusted closed, the mine holes filled with rainwater, melted snow. The exposed gravel gathered dust and bugs and started to form its ecology of dirt and growth. The piles of discarded trees crumpled and rotted. A swampy pond formed, fed by streams and filled with rushes and bullfrogs. Trees grew, feasting upon the bodies of their fallen predecessors. A bobcat moved in. A long-legged crane. A pair of beavers blocked off a narrow part of the pond and built their home. The air smelled rich and green, thick with the calls of songbirds, the buzz of swamp mosquitoes, the croaking of frogs, and the windy swoosh of chest-high grasses.

B and I would walk there sometimes, ducking through a hole in the warning sign–festooned fence and following the grassy lines of what was once tire tracks. I always found bones. I have always been able to find bones. The femurs of deer, scarred by gnawing coyote teeth. Sawed-off chunks from butcher shops stolen from the garbage by crows. The tiny skulls of rodents. On a dry, warm day, bones smell like cement and dirt, like old teeth, like a denser form of driftwood. They smell old but not tired or worn—a yellow-paged book untouched on a shelf, the air in a jar of loose-leaf tea.

When the wind blew right—sometimes on a clear night, sometimes on the hottest of days—you could smell a body in the gravel mine.

WHEN I FIRST met him, the tree man was a gangly, thin-limbed sapling, awkward and bow shouldered and uncertain in the high school hallways of spit and shove and discontent. You can only stand so tall when you have to stoop and curve to fit through doorways, to fit expectations. A young tree in a terra-cotta pot will be stunted, bonsaied if its roots cannot reach and spread. Sometimes, you have to leave and drive east in a blue-striped pickup truck to find suitable space. A migration of one. Window down, elbow in the slipstream breeze, sunlight a soft hand on the shoulder, good music on the speakers. Crank it up, crank it out, gas pedal sinking to the floor, a long-winged bird flying.

The tree man is now tall and solid, at least six foot fifteen, with hands like widespread pine branches. He has grown deep roots, straightened and stretched to match his shoulders. His eyes are stormgrayblue with silver stars; he squints in the sharp sunlight and steps sure-footedly between the doorframes of tree trunks. Surviving becomes thriving when transplanted to appropriate soil.

TODAY, I AM burying a quail hen. House pets—cats and dogs—are cremated and kept indoors where they found their comforts. Random wild animals found deceased on the property are, depending on the state of decomposition and manner of death, either tossed in the forest for scavengers, buried under a random tree, or placed in a wire cage with a brick on top so the bones can be cleaned by rodents and insects and retrieved later for examination, collection, art. As for our honey bees, most of them die while working in the fields, collapsing from old age and exhaustion, and the bees that die inside failed winter hives are too tiny and numerous to bury, so we lay them to rest in the same place they perish in the wild: on the lawn, scattered haphazardly, without ceremony. The quails, though, are neither house pets nor wild animals, so they are buried in a place we are unlikely to walk or dig: around the base of a sprawling rho-dodendron bush.

The blade sinks only halfway into the ground, then stops sharply: the soil is thick, tough, and only a few inches deep. I rock the shovel back, lift the soil, stab again, lift. The blade snags on a root from a blackberry vine that has embraced the rhodo's trunk. I wield the shovel like a spear, chopping and tearing at the root, but the root is thick and fibrous, unyielding. I settle for scraping the dirt like porridge from the sides of a bowl, trying to carve out a hollow big enough to cradle my little bird.

The first quail was buried under the side of the rhodo bush closest to the house; the next, a foot to the right of it, and the next, a foot to the right of that, over the years form-ing a counterclockwise ring-around-the-rosy. The graves are unmarked: What would one write on the gravestone of an animal that had no name. And if every buried corpse were marked with a commemorative stone or stick, within a few years, a farm or acreage would begin to resemble a disorganized graveyard: vaguely morbid, overly reverent, difficult to navigate. It is supposedly rude to step on some-one's grave, though we do so all the time without knowing; thus, it is best to place home burials tucked away under bushes or in corners between trees. But it is easy enough to tell where the most recent quail has been planted: the soil is raised a bit, uneven, and bare of the usual undergrowth of moss and small, tough-leafed plants. They are small, and there are many of them.

WE BURY TO hide.

A dog buries his half-eaten bones for later retrieval. A rabbit buries her young to protect them, in a nest of dried grass and soft fluff ripped from a parent's chest. A child buries their face in their hands, shy and crying, or laughing.

We bury our disappointments, our mistakes, our embarrassments, the things we do not wish to look at or be looked at. We bury our dead to prevent the spread of contagious disease and preserve our memories of them as their bodies decompose.

A child buries themself in blankets, in playfulness or fear of monsters. A soldier buries themself in a dug-out hole, camouflaged and covered. In times of great shame and sorrow, we may wish to bury ourselves, cease being conscious of our own existence, metacognitively implode like a collapsing star. There is much that is caused by fear, by the desire to escape it.

We bury things to pretend they don't exist or to wish they never had.

In a huge hole in spoiled, unsanctified ground in the back of a church, hundreds of bones of small children hastily covered.

AARON'S NOVEL—FICTION, THOUGH the facts feel familiar—is about a town beneath a lake. Once upon a time, there was a valley community, wooden houses with roads and perhaps a cafe or corner store. Snowmobiles, guns against the bears, cases of beer trucked in from the next town over. Then a hydroelectric company moved in to flood the valley for a massive power-generating dam that turned the motion from water-spun turbines into stored, usable electricity to light the rooms of buildings in cities.

The valley residents were ushered out—some graciously, others resisting and reluctant, depending on the depth of their roots—and given large dollars in exchange for relinquishing their lifestyle and land.

Once flooded, the valley formed a large lake, the tips of submerged trees protruding near its shores. The remnants of former roads dipped beneath its surface, going nowhere, to a town that no longer existed. Road signs became gravestones for a disenfranchised and displaced community.

On top of the lake, motorboats roar and float, shiny mechanical toys purchased with the money from selling off old homesteads, houses built by grandparents, family graves. The clink and chirp of wine glasses, celebratory cheers.

Far below the boats' propeller blades, the peaked roofs of houses grow soft and saturated, slick with algae, beginning to decompose. A sunken garage cradles the now-vintage car still parked in it. Random objects forgotten or abandoned during the relocation float to the surface: a dish towel, discolored photographs, a shoe.

THERE IS A certain oily stench to human death. The old farmers and volunteer firefighters in the neighborhood nod their heads knowingly, quietly, when the body in the gravel mine is mentioned. They're familiar with the thick, meaty stench of a half-eaten deer in the forest or of a misplaced chicken that died in a shadowy barn corner and lay undiscovered for days. Press your lips closed and keep your tongue to the roof of your mouth lest you taste the air and gag—but despite its noxiousness, the scent of a decomposing animal is clean, an unapologetic bouquet of biological processes, bugs and bacteria breaking down tissues and fluids into gases, dirt, life. Their bones, once picked clean, smell like a sweeter version of stones, driftwood.

Humans, on the other hand, are heavy with fat and saturated with oils, their guts full of poorly digested food substitutes and their skin coated in the complex chemicals of detergents and toiletries. Factory-made substances with unpronounceable names decompose slow, farting strange-smelling fumes. Human death smells heavy, sour.

The body in the gravel mine cries softly, lost, calling for help. You can sense them when the wind blows across the swamp, feel their bones pull against your sternum. Flies bashing against the window of a stale, closed room. A small child alone in a shopping mall. A rusted car at the bottom of a lake.

There is nothing of logic that could be said to methodical investigators with their dogs and badges and paperwork. How to describe this smell, so subtly different from the wet swamp fumes and the usual odors of fallen trees and rotting carrion. How it lasts for years, fleeting wisps tangled in the autumn mists and rustle of leaves. How the breastbone aches, pulled toward some vague and unknown location within ninety acres of forbidden, fenced space.

The body in the gravel mine calls softly. They have lost their name, their home. They are an unfinished story.

A MIDNIGHT JOYRIDER hyped up on unknown chemicals has sideswipe-smashed one of our apple trees and walked away, disoriented, from a twisted metal car frame and our uprooted tree with broken and exposed roots, a tire caught in its bent branches. I frantically reach out to the tree man with requests for advice on recovery and aftercare, on how to hospitalize and play nurse to a species I don't quite understand.

He nods approvingly at the pulley winch B has used to haul the tree back upright and the two-by-four crutches bracing the tree's trunk and heavy limbs.

"You've done the right things," he says reassuringly. "Give it a layer of fertilizer and water it nonstop for the next week. It will either survive or it won't, in whole or in part. You may not know for another year. Don't prune it this fall; let it heal. It may need its supports in perpetuity."

I point out a twisted and lopsided tree bent at its base, its trunk curved in an *s* as though it had been molded while soft, then shoved into place.

"Why is it so odd," I ask, "when its neighbors of the same size grow straight?"

"Elves," the tree man says solemnly. "They pull and play on a sapling when it is small, and it grows in place like that."

I grumble and glare up at him.

"Social distancing," he says. "Trees are smarter than we are, and when some toxic fungus or problem parasite is going around, they'll sense it and lean away from the infected one. And sometimes, if a tree takes root too close to another, it'll grow parallel to the ground to try to escape the shade, and when it finds a patch of light, it'll bend up and reach for the sun. Or if it's knocked over and survives, it'll heal in place and continue to grow from where it stands. Or if there's oil in the dirt, a tree will get soft and rubbery on hot days—you can shove it into strange shapes, and when the cool night air hits it, it gets locked into place."

"Okay, thanks," I say sincerely—but then I look up and see that sideways glance, that impish, eyebrow-twitch hint of a grin.

THE DIRT I am burying my quail in is shallow, only a few inches deep. Beneath that, a hundred feet of gravel, gravel all the way down until bedrock. Within this crushed rock is the giant underground aquifer we draw our well water from, an infrastructure of pipes and wires to support the neighborhood's houses and the roots of trees.

The gravel is smooth and rounded, ground down and polished over hundreds of years of motion—a rainbow of bluegrays and whites and redbrowns. We are miles from the shoreline, but these stones are ocean rocks, souvenirs of ancient history.

Millennia ago, this region was under the ocean. Tectonic shifts brought what was beneath the water to the surface. The region was covered in glaciers, massive mountains of packed snow crushed into ice like coal into diamonds. As the earth shifted and slowly warmed, the glaciers melted, shrinking and slipping downhill into the valleys between the mountains, sliding and draining toward the ocean.

As they moved, the ice dragged with it rocks, stones, and bones from the mountains and valleys they covered, like wet feet on a sandy beach carrying granules from one footstep to the next. The sliding pressure of the moving glaciers dragged a mélange of quartz, slate, limestone, and the petrified bones of ancient sea creatures, ground them down so they became crushed and rounded into smaller pieces with smooth surfaces. And like sand-coated feet walking from a beach, the glaciers scattered their confetti of collected multicolored stones as they moved, creating trails of gravel from the mountain valleys to the ocean.

The sliding glaciers left in their wake mountain lakes, gravel-lined riverbeds, snaking lines from the higher elevations to the ocean. And on the damp gravel there grew mosses, lichens, tiny plants, and colonies of bugs that multiplied and died, their excrement and decomposing bodies forming a thick layer of nutrient-rich grime for the next generation of plants and creatures to live in and subsist on. And the next, and the next, thousands of years of growing and eating and shitting and dying and decomposing piling up to form an ever-richer, ever-thicker layer of soil. Beneath the soil, the detritus of glaciers. Within the soil, a complex ecology of bacteria, dirt-dwelling rodents, bugs, and worms, the roots and rhizomes of plants and trees. And on top of it, I stand with my shovel, tangled in blackberry vines and rhododendron branches, stabbing ineffectively at the earth.

"AARON," I SAY. "Am I remembering that part of your book correctly, or have I told myself the story of the town beneath the lake so many times that I painted motorboats and clinking glasses into the scene, imagined a floating shoe where there was nothing? I have flipped through your book over and over trying to find it, but I don't know what to look for. Am I remembering something that exists, or am I manifesting it from guesses and misinterpretations?"

Aaron doesn't remember. He has written so much since that the details of long-ago writings have grown blurred and indistinct, overlaid by years of other research and editing. He says he'd have to flip through his original manuscript or a copy of the published book. And both are buried in a box of other books, in a stack somewhere; it would take some digging to find.

EVERY YEAR, PEOPLE go missing. To be missing, a person must be separated from their expected location and schedule, their absence noticed by others. To be missing is to be unexpectedly dis-connected—a state of being that necessitates first having been connected: to others, to a home, to land, to a place in time. Those who roam, or who were thrown or stolen from their location, those who had their roots and social ties broken or torn from them, those who are alone—they can disappear, and their vacancy may be unacknowledged, unnoticed, unknown. An absence can only exist if a state of presence is first respected.

If only there was a highway somewhere where young hitchhikers stuck out their thumbs and vanished. If only there were organized gangs that dealt in disapproved products and policed each other's movements with purloined guns and violence. If only there were urban hermits living on the thin strings of sidewalk existence. If only there were displaced Indigenous Peoples seeking the scattered graves of their ancestors. If only there were a list of missing women, children, and two-spirited people. An absence can only exist if a state of presence is first acknowledged.

If only there was a missing-person poster with a photograph and a name. If only there was a numbered folder in a filing cabinet somewhere with a clue pointing toward the area of the gravel mine. If only there was someone missing.

Would it be worth it for the police to dig up and sift through tons of tree-covered, swampy soil in search of the knucklebone or rib of some anonymous person who may or may not be missed. Who would decide, and based on what guidelines. How does one determine the value, the worth, of a person while pretending a socioeconomic hierarchy does not exist. How much are you willing to spend on an anonymous and whispering ghost. Is it worth it, perhaps, to search for an absent person who was never officially present.

The farmers and firefighters nod their heads solemnly, recognizing the scent of the body in the gravel mine, knowing the lost.

WE BURY THINGS to get rid of them, to make them go away. Large urban centers with more people than space ship their garbage to a rural area outside of town and pile it up in great, festering heaps. When the heaps get too tall, or the city spreads too close, they level the heaps, bury them in dirt and grass seed, and reinvent it into a green space. How ironic that what was once wild becomes first a city's most dishonored address, then is repurposed and cherished as urban development spreads slowly around it.

We bury our memories to forget them. A recollection that is thought of repeatedly becomes reinforced, strengthened, thickened like layers of paint added to a canvas. But a memory that is avoided weakens and fades. The mind flinches and skitters away from that which we find embarrassing, awkward, sad—we let that memory fade and paint over it with new imaginings, daydreams, the stories of what could have been, until they are so detailed we mistake them for reality.

We bury something to make the thing, the memory of the thing, and its effects go away.

We bury toxic waste in massive metal containers, concrete blocks deep in the earth or the ocean. Don't crack that barrel—the effluent will spill out and poison you. Don't think of that day—the guilt will break you. Bury the past, the hurt. An unmarked mass grave of misplaced children. A dirty, tear-streaked face. Thick chemicals oozing into an underground stream. A cat defecates, buries it, wipes his paws without looking back, moves on.

I PRY MY shovel into the thin ground, lift, and see the unmistakable flop of a bit of dark fabric. I curse quietly, dump the dirt back into place, and tamp the soil down with the backside of the shovel blade. I have apparently come full circle, buried a full ring of bird bodies around the rhododendron bush.

B is not home for me to ask if I can bury the quail under another bush or tree; he would not say no, but I don't want to risk digging up some important wire or pipe or a family pet that passed before my arrival. I shove my way farther into the cloud of rhodo branches and again stab my shovel into the ground.

What can be grown in such shallow soil anyway? Not a garden: My modest plot is in boxes that were placed on top of the earth and filled with wheelbarrows of dirt. What could grow here? Blackberries, certainly. The wild vines that infest the edges of the local forests are fast growing and determined and will likely take over the property once we leave if it is unmaintained for any summer months before the developers start work.

THE GRAVEL PIT is bulldozed now, the beaver pond and coyote dens and deer nests leveled in preparation for future houses and corner stores, the animal bones and seashells and stumps of trees and enigmatic corpse churned up and reburied helter-skelter. And our property and the quail bones, the misplaced gardening tools, the remnants of old fence posts will be bulldozed and uprooted, too, scattered and reburied under imported dirt and cement and wire, topped with huge houses with perfect, postage-stamp lawns. And, I assume, a quota amount of tall greenery.

I picture the property lines with dull, identical trees, blocks upon blocks of urban monoculture. And when those trees shed their leaves or break and fall, and it is all carted away tidily instead of being allowed to rot into the earth, how will that affect the composition of the soil. Do trees grow best in dirt composed of their own relatives' flesh or that of others. What mosses will grow on their trunks. What birds will nest in their branches. If you build a row of identical houses, will only one kind of family move into them—and where does everyone else go. Are there reserves or replacement housing for the displaced, for those that no longer fit in.

The tree man assures me that there are rules and regulations about this. There are those who have studied such things, the projected effects of the planting of species and the importance of biodiversity. He says the developers and arborists have to adhere to certain guidelines for providing green spaces and planting trees and shrubs. He does not say: It will be fine.

But. Anxious-eyed and skeptical, I second-guess the expert. What kind of greenery can be expected to replace the lush and diverse ecology of the wild forests and our lawn full of weeds and their accessory native bugs and bees. Would the incoming houses be divided by thin rows of blue-tipped pricklepines, or would their lawns be lined with EasyCare PrettyBushes™. Would the needleshedding flakebarks and pollenbomb sapdrippers be delegated to city parks or removed entirely for being too messy and inconvenient. Would fruit and nut trees be in the mix, or do such things grow exclusively in orchards. Would any of the current native greenery be saved or replaced, or would it all, like our house and fence and pithy, pun-covered signposts, be removed or bulldozed into the soil.

"I am sorry," the tree man says, "I don't know. We provide only specific services for certain clients." He says he has a book, somewhere, of charts and statistics and official regulated guidelines. He says it is buried with other papers from the past in a box in storage. He says he will dig it out if he has the time. He does not say: It will be fine.

I AM DIGGING a bramble-haloed hole to bury my quail, a thin breeze from the gravel mine at my back. The wildland habitat of the gravel mine is no longer present, has ceased to exist.

Allegedly, old, closed mines must be bulldozed, demolished, and re-soiled to allow Nature to reclaim them. There is no deadline for this task—four months or forty years after the last truckload of gravel or gold was hauled out, days or decades after the trees grow and the coyotes dig their dens. On paper, the intent does not appear to be to treat the rural ecology fairly and gently—but rather to bury the past, to erase the digging of holes and the mining of resources as though they'd never happened. How convenient that in the center of a rural neighborhood slated for rezoning from farmland and fields into condos and townhouse complexes, it is easier to sell and develop freshly flattened land than a raw and lumpy forest. Old, closed mines must be bulldozed to allow Nature to reclaim them, supposedly.

The truck tire tracks overgrown with weeds, thigh-thick trees, snarls of blackberry brambles and tiny-leafed shrubbery, the decades-old furrows and holes forming lush, muddy marshes of muskrats, cranes, and beaver dams. The spring-melt creek of wriggling minnows. The lost and softly calling bones of the unknown body. The coyote dens, deer nests. It has all been choked back, pulled down, and cut under by chainsaws and backhoes and large, noisy trucks spreading dust and beeping cacophony. Flattened and barren. New sandy soil has been trucked in from elsewhere, piled in great beige mountains and spread out like bland putty, like matte off-white paint over wallpaper. The bones have been broken and disassembled, scattered and churned under and tamped down by heavy machinery. A flat new beginning.

WE BURY TO nourish, to fertilize. That which is buried and decomposes becomes the soil that nourishes new life. From corpse to dirt to the growth of plants to our mouths and the mouths of the animals we eat. Banana peels and eggshells folded into flower beds balance soil biochemistry and protect from pests. A layer of old leaves on rose bulbs forms a protective mulch against winter cold and nourishes spring growth. A post-spawn, washed-up, rotting salmon tucked into the garden makes the best tomatoes. The childhood afternoons I spent collecting fish beside the lake were not appreciated: sullenly trudging behind my mother along the shoreline, lugging a stinking garbage bag and shovel, embarrassed and avoiding meeting the neighbors' eyes, opportunistically gathering the dead.

There is a slow process to this, a cycle that must be patiently respected. Skipping a step results in twisted bellies and flinching faces. Pigs fed dead fish shortly before slaughter produce sour bacon. Chickens given a last meal of freezer-burnt sausage make for foul barbecued wings. Such stinking mistakes can only be fed to dogs or buried, because Nature is a stern supervisor who insists you go back and repeat any steps you missed. The babies that are buried badly in the backyards of churches will cry until we find them, bring them home, and name them.

THERE IS A myth that untouched nature exists in a perfect and constant state of stasis. It has its cycles of change and waves that ebb and flow, but it always revolves around and returns to a central point of balance. An analog clock that never ceases rotating and with each moment displays a different time but itself remains unchanged. A pendulum that swings in consistent movement, continually repeating the same steps of its simple dance, constantly changing position yet remaining unchanged.

Into this pastoral perfection came barging the great upsetter of stability: European settlers, *Homo industrious progressive,* who, rather than heeding the traditional knowledge of Indigenous Peoples, custodians of the land they colonized, arrived like otherworld aliens with their guns and machinery and chemicals and computers, throwing Nature's perfection into discordant tragedy and chaos.

And Nature reacted in anger, throwing temper tantrums of heat waves and tidal waves, shaking the tectonic plates with earthquakes and raising the ocean levels, threatening to drown the lot of them. If *H. industrious progressive* does not stop, does not reverse the changes it has made to this previously pristine system, Nature will self-destruct, taking the invaders with it.

Or so the myth goes.

BUT NATURE IS not fully formed and stable; it does not resist, rise up, and rebel like a human would. Nature is a complex system of constant evolution. It adopts, absorbs, adapts. It does not crumble; it changes. It is present and mutable, and we are not apart from it—we are a part of it.

A patch of earthy land that has a truckful of sand added to it does not cease to exist, does not somehow become not-dirt. It becomes sandy dirt. The plants that grow in it, the animals that burrow in it, and its ability to hold and filter water change. It is not destroyed; it is different. So, too, for a truckload of industrial gravel instead of sand—or shredded plastic, paint-coated wood chips, or iridescent chemical effluent. The inhabiting species relocate or die off and are replaced by others, or not. Even a barren, oil-saturated patch of land is not destroyed. It has not somehow ceased to exist. It has changed. And we can have our judgments about whether we desire such changes or not, whether we wish to continue to influence Nature's evolution in this direction or not.

THIS LAND IS not ours to sell. Pieces of paper say it is, but there was never a piece of paper that certified a transfer of ownership from the Indigenous Peoples who lived here to the European colonizers who moved in and took up residence in this space. As legal owners selling and moving away, we are guests leaving, making way for more uninvited guests.

Beneath our feet, the remnants of thousands of years of inhabitants have been churned up, crushed, mixed into the soil, and lost. The bones of the dead, pieces of housing and clothing, garbage and souvenirs and misplaced toys, woven baskets, stone tools, all crushed and broken and decomposed, each new onslaught of machinery and paperwork cutting new lines into old, lost history. The fragments of things left behind break down into new soil. I knock a clump of dirt from my shovel and wonder how much of it was someone's favorite toy or well-worn clothing, the unknown origin of a broken stone I've unearthed.

MY QUAIL HAS died, succumbed to rats or disease or age. The shovel does not cut deeply enough: beneath the topsoil, a heavy gravel of round stones worn smooth, river rock, ocean stone. This region was once all under water, then glaciers. Now, the seas have shrunk, lifted the land dry. The great hand of geographic evolution spread dirt over it all, as though it could bury a memory of the ocean. Now, there are houses, and power lines, and trees, and me.

WE BURY THE bones of our ancestors, our selves, and dig them up again, by accident or intent, scatter and rebury them, in a grand and endless process of claiming and creating and relinquishing the dirt. Our bones become the earth. We can never let them go; we can only decompose and hope something grows from them.

The decomposition of the detritus of our species is slow. Bodies and plants buried in the earth break down in weeks or months, perhaps longer if chemically preserved, but unlike pine needles and feathers, our sheddings decompose sluggishly.

Like the small shards of fallen bones and smashed stones, the buried bits of things we leave behind become homogenized into the earth, changing the texture of the soil and the biological composition of that which can grow from it. The buildings grow taller. The green spaces grow smaller. The ecology evolves.

THE TREE MAN wanders around our property and comments congenially on the neglected butterfly bush and off-kilter lilac trees. He pokes his head into the canopies of the gnarled, twisted apple trees and offers pruning advice, pointing out the tiny buds of new bending branches and where to angle my clippers to entice the best fruit yield. He grins, looking mischievously down at me from the corner of his eye.

"If you dump a load of manure or compost on their roots, they'll love it," he says.

I remind him that in a few years, this will all be gone, bulldozed. There's not much point in long-term projects like reshaping the lilac bushes or coercing the apple trees into decades of fruit. We can't take them with us, and no one is going to save some old trees of unknown species. They'll likely get ripped up, dragged around by big machinery, thrown into a wood chipper. All we can do is take care of them in the meantime.

The tree man pauses between two trees, stretches his arms out, and presses palms against bark. He is Samson, shoving the pillars, my world falling down around and on top of him. I imagine that if he stands too long in one place, he'll stretch into the ground and sky, bark rippling up his legs, fingers spreading leaves as though under an enchantment. He sighs, squints into the sunlight, and moves on.

WE BURY TO forgive.

Forgiveness is an often mis-cited concept. To forgive is not to erase, walk away, pretend no harm has happened. It is not embracing an enemy or abuser, pressing your chest against theirs, laughing in stilted friendship as lingering wounds bleed and fester. It is not crumpling up and tossing away a written list of wrongdoings. It is not covering a scab or crack, hiding a scar. It is not an erasure of the past.

To forgive is to accept. To forgive is to relinquish a clinging hold on the past, to let it go and watch it slip down and away like a heavy chained anchor uncoiling from a pile and falling down through the water. To acknowledge what has been done, what has happened. To forgive is to accept that it is out of your hands, gone, unchangeable.

We bury not to change but to accept. That which is buried in the earth stays with the earth, becomes part of it.

We dig up and rebury the bones of children. They are so small, and there are so many of them.

THE EXODUS OF the characters in Aaron's novel echoes that of the Indigenous Peoples who were slaughtered or relocated to make way for European immigrants. Now, our farmland neighborhood is being scouted by aggressively smiling, vulture-eyed developers and rezoned from semi-agricultural to higher-density housing. The old houses soften and decompose below the water, below the boats. The buildings grow; below them, the soil and souvenirs of our histories. The trading of a lifestyle of tree bark and steel-toed gumboots for arbitrary numbers that can change a life, be squandered, or exchanged for temporary luxuries. Is this beneficial for all involved, or is it a handful of cheap glass beads, a fistful of magic beans. The men pick up their tools and move to where the work is.

DRAW A MAP of this land, this town, this region. Mark on it all the locations of notable moments, both joys and horrors. This is where we met. This is where we found the stones. Here is where we drove over broken glass, shreds of neon caution tape, a smear on the asphalt. Here is the diner with the delicious thick waffles. There was the heron that flew up from a field.

Mark the locations of all the graves, both those known and not. Draw a map of tragedy. Of history.

Spread the map flat, draw lines. Tell the stories geographically. The connections of experiences. When you can map your past across time and space, you know where you are: here and now in relation to where and when you have been.

Emulate the bulldozers, the destruction, the rearrangement of hundreds of future years. Shred the map into pieces. Crumple and mix them. Spread them out, press them flat to form a new map. All the lines are disconnected, the locations rearranged. Build new layers on top: landmarks, locations, culture. Add organic experience, activity, life in motion.

Tell me who you are in this. Where do you fit in? Where do you go when where you have been no longer exists. Do you only have memories, punctuated by random souvenirs. Memories are like photographs: fallible, malleable. Souvenirs fall apart, are lost, fall out of context, are buried in boxes and not seen again.

THE GRAVE IS as deep as I can make it and wide enough to fit a tiny body.

I place the quail hen in her grave, carefully tucking the bit of old bedsheet around her to ensure nothing—not feathered wing nor open beak nor tiny clawed foot—is left exposed. As though a dead animal could get cold, or cared. It is tradition to say a small prayer, but I do not know what religion farmyard animals ascribe to, so instead I say a soft goodbye while resting my palm on her covered body, fingers curving around her little bent neck, soft, feathered breast, short tail, and awkwardly angled legs.

"Goodbye," I whisper. "I hope I have given you a good life."

I dump the dirt over her, pat it down with the shovel, and add a few scoops of eggshell-riddled black soil from the bottom of the compost bin for good measure. I soak the grave down with the hose for several minutes: to settle the soil, to disguise the smell of death that may attract four-pawed foragers, to kickstart the process of decay.

A few years from now, after we have sold the property and moved on, this will all be bulldozed: the house, B's workshop, the toolshed, and the garage. The few remaining trees with their accessory birdhouses, the vicious blackberry vines, my garden boxes full of rogue tomatoes and squash. The millions of dead bees from dozens of hives scattered on the lawn and mingling with the earth. The rhododendron bush with its dirty halo of quail graves.

I imagine some steel-toed backhoe operator unearthing a shred of colored fabric and noticing within it tiny bones, a fistful of feathers. Would they think it evidence of some pagan ritual, recognize its location and significance, or think it just more random garbage. We will have moved on. These are the things we will leave behind.

Things I Have Unearthed While Digging Holes

A FLAT BLACK STONE with a seashell embedded in it. Blackberry roots. Plastic tags from bread bags. Brittle slabs of slate. Chunks of broken glass. An ant nest. Cat's-eye marbles. Smashed eggshells. Flat, pliable fridge magnets. Round, melted-glass pebbles from the bottom of a fish tank.

A copper-colored stone. A shiny, oblong jewel. Soda pop cans. Forgotten potatoes. Closed plastic bags with decomposed, unknown contents.

A raccoon jaw. A flap of fabric from a T-shirt. Huge larvae. The rusted blade of a garden trowel.

Shredded plastic. Hagstones. Wet, slippery gray clay. Severed wires, their metal exposed. A red rubber dog's toy. A thick, moldy clump, likely excrement.

Dusty chunks of limestone. The skulls of rats. Bottle caps. Rabbit leg bones.

A surprising pocket of sand. A tiny yellow dump truck. The spine of a book. Spiders carrying egg sacs. Discarded cat litter, slippery and gritty. A tiny pink doll's shoe. The eggs of unknown insects. Deer ribs. The roots of trees. Pieces of cement. A giant beetle with bulbous abdomen.

Coins. Chunks of quartz crystal. The roots of grass, dandelions, thistles. Dirt. Stones. Bones.

Beyond Science

IMAGINE A HUGE space full of many things, like a universe full of the dots of planets and stars. Within this space is a small, blurry-edged circle with many dots and speckles inside of it. These represent the things we know, like science. The things beyond the circle, beyond our current understanding, are what we call religion or spirituality. We invent theories, ideas, and complex systems of belief to attempt to explain what we do not know based on what little we do. Or we simply pretend that the unknown things do not exist.

The blurry, indefinite area between science and religion encapsulates the things we cannot yet explain. Here is where ghosts live, and intuition, and unexplained phenomena. This is the area of magic or, as it is commonly called, scientific exploration, experimentation, and research. It will always be subject to criticism and ridicule.

Experiences in this area can be difficult to examine. We look at them sideways, from the corner of a cautious eye, and talk about them quietly, cautiously, feeling vulnerable and uncertain. Or we speak of them like myths, like twice-told tales, like stories that happened to a friend of a friend, a distant and nameless third person.

GRANNY, MY TINY and ancient mother-in-law, lives in the mobile home down the road, past the house where B and I live with our honey bees and assorted pets. She drives with head cocked to one side as she passes our house, eyes toward its fenced-in yard in case the dog is doing his hourly patrol of the yard's perimeter.

Inside the house, the dog's ears cock at the sound of tires. He runs to the door, startling the cat, begs to be let out, clears the porch, and sprints along the fence line, yelling with joy.

Granny stops, steps out of her car, and leans over the fence to rub the dog's ears and hand him treats.

One day a decade from now, I will be emptying Granny's home: setting aside certain things for the children and grandchildren, packing the rest up for charity. Beside the pool of boxes in progress—lumpy sweaters and folded pants, books, photos, canned food, dishes carefully wrapped in tea towels—is the rocking chair where she would sit for hours.

I will lift a box intending to set it on the chair's seat—but suddenly sense intense anger, rejection. Instead, I will set the box to one side and pull the chair from the corner, into the light, beside where I am working. The alarming feeling will fade, and I will imagine the old woman laughing.

For months, I will work beside the chair: sorting, packing, cleaning. Never again will I attempt to set boxes on the chair, on Granny's lap. One evening, I will spend several hours cleaning the back room, out of sight of the chair. When I emerge, the chair will be facing the back room. It will rock slightly, as though someone had just sat down or stood up.

GRANNY IS OLDER now. She has not driven past the house in years. She has not driven in years. The dog, now older, too, sleeps on the couch in the house, gray muzzled and slowing. When tires crunch on the gravely road, he no longer leaps and barks—his eyes are fading, his ears full of fog and the memories of sounds.

The dog sleeps in the sunbeam and dreams of chasing rabbits, paws twitching, whining. Down the road, Granny dozes in her armchair, dreams of sunrises over oceans, her hands folded softly, remembering. The fat, lazy cat, curled up by the dog, watches the road through the window like a small, silent sentry.

One day a few years from now, there will be no dog, only random bits of fur still tumbled into lesser-swept corners and under appliances. When B and I sit at our desks or at the dining table, we will sometimes feel rough fur brush against our legs or a damp snout resting on our foot. We will reach down without thinking, then remember, look down, and convince ourselves we felt nothing.

SOME PEOPLE ASSUME that all other creatures are inferior to us humans in intellect. They assume animals' cognitive skills are limited, their values and belief systems are rudimentary, and their philosophies and spiritual beliefs are nonexistent. Why? Because animals do not appear to have industry, technology, or complex economies that we can recognize? It is entirely possible that other creatures have developed ologies beyond our comprehension, values, and ways of thinking and being that are as foreign and beyond our understanding as our systems of political government and institutionalized religion are to a rabbit.

Some cultures hold other states of consciousness in as high regard as conscious thought. They pick apart dreams, analyze visions and hallucinations, and interpret perceived symbolic messages with as much consideration and respect as one would give conscious communication between awake and alive people.

We assume animals have the uneducated mentalities of small children. We use adult humans as the measuring stick by which we gauge all other creatures, and where they differ from us, we deem them lacking. When a pet startles awake from a particularly dramatic dream, we assume that, like a small child, they are confused and disoriented, unable to differentiate between dreams and reality.

How arrogant of us.

Perhaps animals can perceive things we don't. Nonlinear time. Alternative states of being. The presence of those who are no longer recognized as *alive*. Perhaps, like some human cultures, animals have a complex relationship with the dream world, with the otherworld, with layers of being and beings that science has yet to discover or explain.

Given all this, consider how animals might perceive death. Are they aware it exists as part of their future. Are they afraid of it. How do they perceive the dead. Are they alarmed by the dead, or is our own fear of such merely the product of our arbitrary systems of belief, of our rudimentary science and interpretative religions.

GRANNY SLEEPS WITHOUT waking in a sterile hospital bed miles away, her breath slowing. She is moving beyond dreams, beyond the soft murmur of conversation around her. B and his children sit around her and wait, watch, count her breaths. They say Important Things.

B returns to the house, to me and the cat and the old dog. We eat our meals, doze in chairs. The house creaks and settles in the cooling evening.

At a quarter to nine, the lazy cat startles and runs down the hall, fur spiked like protective armor, paws skidding around corners. The dog barks, jumps up from the couch, and runs to the door, howling like fireworks. B staggers up from his nap, opens the door, and watches as the dog runs along the fence by the road, tail wagging, barking, and howling joyfully into the empty night.

B leans against the doorway, crosses his arms, squints. "I think that was her," he says. "I think that was her saying goodbye."

I nod in agreement.

Ten past nine, the phone rings. B answers, speaking calmly. I arch an eyebrow. He meets my eye and nods. Granny is gone, found breathless and silent a few minutes ago.

One day years from now, the deer and coyotes and birds and rats that inhabit the property will all have passed on. The rabbits the dog chased will all have long since passed on; their generations of offspring will also be gone.

AMID THE ZEN and loveliness of agriculture and owning pets, the reality of dealing with animals is that sometimes they die. Or have to be killed. Kindness is sometimes a firm hand and a heavy heart.

When you adopt an animal, you are signing up to kill them. You will almost certainly outlive them, so one day, you will have to make the decision of when they should die. Give them a good life. But also give them a good death: gentle and timely, without unnecessary suffering. If their last moments are in a strange-smelling place full of needles and strangers, be there with them and hold them as they go, for they are confused and scared, and you are their home and comfort. If you are not willing to do this, you should not keep animals. Your pets give you joy and love and comfort—and you clean up their accidental messes, and you give them joy, love, and, when it's time, a comforting goodbye.

It is never easy or pleasant. You stand in your home or the veterinary clinic or your yard by the roadside, with disheveled clothes and a blotchy face of snot and tears, a howling hollow in your gut. When someone so vulnerable is suffering, the need to give them dignity and comfort is so intense that you must sacrifice your own.

Creatures die. It's the reality of agriculture. Even bee colonies die. You clean up the mess and move on, without fanfare. But there's a difference between a death that's out of your control and having to deliberately euthanize a being you've developed a relationship with—for mercy or to prevent the spread of disease and fatality. There is no veterinarian that will administer end-of-life shots to your bees while you hold their little paws. It's hands-on. You are the agent of death, administering silence to something living that cannot understand. It doesn't matter how many broken bird necks you've twisted or lawnmower-mangled snakes you've crushed—it doesn't get easier. Take the old horse out back, look it in the eye, and put a gun to its forehead. If you don't grit your teeth against tears and stare a hundred yards into the horizon, you just don't fucking care. You pick up your tools, wash your face with cold, cold water, and move on.

GRANNY RESTS IN her urn of cremains on the bookshelf. The cat has grown lazier. The dog moves slowly, stiff with arthritis, ribs thinning with hidden cancers. He has not run around the perimeter of the yard in months. He walks slowly from his bed toward the door, rests for several minutes, rises and walks again, rests, and eventually reaches the door. B and I talk quietly, sincerely, about how long his life will be, and when it will end.

The dog does not notice when the cat steals his food; his ears are silent, his eyes stormgray with cataracts. The cat grows fatter. The dog moves slowly, sleeps.

One day, B and I will move away, taking with us the cremains and souvenirs and memories of our dead. We will not return. We will not visit our old home with its buried bones and collection of ghosts. We will leave, driving away without looking over our shoulders, uncertain whether we are leaving anything behind.

DO THE DEAD stay connected to specific locations, to their physical remains, or to the living beings to whom they are emotionally attached. How long do they stay. Do they move on or dissipate. Does three-dimensional space become a non sequitur. Is linear time (ir)relevant. When pets die, where do they stay—with their owners or with their homes. When *home* changes, when people relocate, do the ghosts get left behind.

And what happens when wild animals die. Do they stay connected to the space they inhabited or the place they died. If they migrated or traversed expansive hunting grounds, do they continue to follow their trails and, if so, for how long.

On a mild evening, one can see a dozen cottontail rabbits grazing on this property. But over the centuries, there have been thousands. Are they all still here, layering and overlapping with each other, scattering under the hooves of herds of ghostly deer and the shadows of long-gone hawks. And if so, are they surprised by the presence of all the fish that lived here when this land was under water. Or is it just the recently deceased that remain: temporary, in transition, fading, dissipating. Where do they go when they go. How long do they stay.

ONE EARLY MORNING, B departs for work, leaving me and the cat and the old dog still sleeping. We will wake in our own time, in hours. The door shuts quietly. A half hour passes.

The cat stands in the bedroom doorway calling, unusually loud and persistent. I stumble from bed; the cat runs down the hallway and hides. I find the dog at the door, waiting silently. I open the door, and he steps out stiffly.

Awake too early, I dish out food for the cat, coffee for myself. The cat stays hidden. I squint out the window to see if the dog is ready to come back in.

He is lying down in a far corner of the yard. Not close to the porch, where he lately squats and scratches, nor along the fence where Granny used to give him treats. The farthest corner of the yard, away from the house, away from recent familiar scents, beyond any distance he has walked in months, away.

I know what this is. I step into the morning chill and crouch by the dog to be with him. A dying animal will leave its pack and venture off alone. I will not leave him alone. I rest a hand on his chest. Breath. Labored, heaving breath. It is raining, gently. I will not leave him alone. But it is cold and raining, and he is so very frail.

The old dog thumps his tail on the ground and rises slowly, stiffly. He walks back to the house—such a long distance for such slow, stiff legs—with me by his side.

Inside, I dish out extra food for him: the soft kind, with extra gravy. He laps at it, tail wagging, but only eats a little. He continues his slow, pausing walk back to his bed, then when he reaches it, he turns and heads for the door again.

I make a rare phone call to B at work. "It is time," I say. I phone the veterinarian. "It is time," I say. And the old dog continues his slow, restless pacing from bed to door and back, never quite reaching either, back and forth, chest heaving with labored breath.

I hang up the phone. The cat is still hiding. The dog finally reaches the door, lies down, thumps his tail weakly.

We step outside. I stand on the porch and watch as the dog steps off it and walks a few feet along the fence line, following the path he used to patrol when he had younger legs.

The old dog stops, looks back with sightless eyes, perks his silent ears toward me. His dry nose twitches.

I walk over to him. He wags his tail once, then continues his trek, me by his side, along the fence line to the corner where Granny would give him treats. He pauses, nose high, then continues. Past the posts, around the next corner, the whole perimeter of his outdoor domain. Such a long walk in the cold, light rain, the longest he has walked in months. He stops every few feet, head turning and sniffing the ghosts of rabbits and the memory of deer, but he never lies down.

He reaches the porch, chest heaving and legs trembling, and pauses. I reach down to pick him up—but he hoists himself onto the porch, into the house. He pauses at his food dish for a last lick of gravy, then continues through the house, never stopping until he reaches his bed.

He lies quietly, chest spasming with breath, finally calm after a morning of restless pacing. He does not raise his head until B returns, kneels, wraps his arms around him in an embrace, and lifts him.

One day a few days from now, I will be holding the cat, pressing a sad cheek against soft fur as we watch the wild rabbits through the window. I will imagine, or think I imagine, the soft thump and metallic jingle of the dog leaping onto the couch and rattling his collar. The cat will turn her head, ears perked, and stare at the empty couch.

THE CAR'S TIRES crunch on the driveway gravel. Inside the car are me, B, and the old dog. From the window of the house, the cat watches as the car turns, pauses, and drives away.

Perhaps she waits for our return and will be confused when the dog remains absent, and she will search for him, querulously mewing, for months. Or perhaps she understands and knows we will return without him, or that he will return, bright-eyed and energetic, before we do.

One day a year from now, the cat will bat toys down the hall, chasing and pouncing on her new kitten companion, surprisingly frisky for a chunky senior cat. The next day, the kitten will meow too much, and the old cat will be unusually quiet and hiding. I will find the old cat curled up, wild-eyed and acid smelling, her ears unusually hot, under my desk. She will try to hide, seeking escape, comfort, rest. B and I will hold her close and say goodbye, and we will give her these.

The next day, the cat's last scoop of kibbles will still be in her little dish. It will stay where it is until someone else eats the kibbles. Her fur-clotted brush will stay as it is until someone uses it to brush the kitten and absent-mindedly cleans it.

I will intend to vacuum and scrub the throw rug under my desk where the old cat had one last messy accident. But I will catch a glimpse, from the corner of my eye, of the cat curling up in her nest box in the kitchen, tucking her face under her paw, her soft brown fur distinct against the crisp-white wall. The cat does not like the vacuum cleaner. I will close the door to my office before vacuuming, and I will only vacuum that room. There is no logical reason for any of this. But some things, like love or comfort, are beyond science.

One day, I will be holding the kitten, watching the rabbits through the window, and the chair where the old cat used to sit will thump and creak as though someone small had leapt onto it. The kitten and I will look toward the empty chair, small hearts racing, ears listening to the memories and the silence.

Fawn

The air is silent and wide, the sunlight still hours away. Inside, B is eating breakfast and reading a book before going to work. He pays little attention to the sounds of the occasional car that drives by on the road: some purr by smooth and steadily, others rattle and clunk, grumbling and halting. Early risers similarly off to morning work, or night owls returning from graveyard shifts or late parties. One car sputters by, a muffled thump, then continues on. B turns a page in his book, takes another bite of his breakfast.

In his car, B starts his engine and pulls out of the driveway. His headlights pass over an unfamiliar shape at the edge of our yard beside the road.

It is the fawn, crumpled and broken.

He kneels beside them, cups a hand in front of their nose—but there is no warm breath, only the chill, pre-dawn air. The fawn's wide, dark eye stares up, reflecting starlight. Their fading white spots of infancy are still visible in their fur. He knows that the doe is somewhere nearby, likely spooked away when he started the car. She is probably watching him from the forest, watching him kneel beside her baby.

If the impact of the car had only flung the fawn a dozen feet farther, or if the fawn had survived long enough to stagger into the forest, they would be hidden by trees instead of lying exposed by the roadside. The doe would be able to grieve and say goodbye to her offspring without being interrupted by passing cars, pedestrians. The following night, after the body was cold and stiff and the doe had moved on, the coyotes would have a meal of fresh carrion, likely accompanied by predatory night birds. Then the rats would arrive, picking and gnawing at the remnants. Then the mice and beetles and wasps, breaking down the last bits until only bone and sinew was left to sink into the earth, decomposing and nourishing the forest plants.

At night, the forest is a sanctuary of hidden safety for wild animals. Not so for humans. Without light, or knowledge of the terrain, humans are blind and lost beneath the tree canopy. Thick snarls of blackberry vines lash at limbs, tearing clothing and cutting skin. The uneven ground of fallen branches and exposed roots trip feet, twist bones. Human bodies are noisy, clumsy. There is folklore about such places. Do not enter at night. Do not go there alone. Do not follow a strange animal into the woods, for that is a lure sent by the fairy folk, and you will not come out again. Human beings are vulnerable. The night forest is not our domain.

From within this darkened otherworld the doe watches, unseen and hidden, watches as the human touches her quiet and unmoving baby.

B rests his hand on the fawn's still-warm neck. He strokes them gently, speaks quietly.

This is not the forest, the space of cycles and life and death and rebirth. This is the roadside, the yard's edge, the space of humans and machines. In a few hours, the sun will rise, the road will become busier. Some driver or pedestrian or neighbor will call the wildlife rescue or the city hall. A truck will arrive; municipal workers in coveralls and gloves will unceremoniously throw the baby into the back of a truck and take them to a rendering plant, where they will be processed into fertilizer or disposed of as garbage.

The fawn stares at the stars. The doe watches from the forest. The air is silent and wide, sunlight still hours away.

As gently as picking up a sleeping child or a beloved pet, B slides his arms under the fawn's body and gathers them to his chest. Carrying them, he walks into the darkness of the forest.

Pandora's Boxes

Winter is the waiting season. The watching season. The season of hope and quiet trepidation. Will the bees survive. Will they be warm enough, clustered together in their tight bundle of tiny bodies within the hive. Will they be able to move around and access food. In a cold snap, will they slip into a self-preserving torpor to conserve energy, or will they simply freeze. On a warm day, will they stay safely clustered or mistake it for spring and move about freely, then succumb to the crashing cold of nightfall.

"How are your bees?" friends ask, and you fumble and stutter, inventing a noncommittal answer. Opening a hive to inspect it in the winter cold would subvert the work the bees do to stay warm and comfortable, and it could kill them. And there's nothing you could do in the winter to address any health issues they may be having anyway, so inspecting is pointless. They exist in limbo, Schrödinger's bees, simultaneously both viable and dying until otherwise confirmed.

You wait and watch the hives through the windows of your house, disconnected from the hands-on warmth and interaction of working with active hives in the summer. As though you were the one in a box, and the bees were somewhere beyond, unreachable.

Occasionally, you see a few bees flying out of a hive, momentarily leaving the warmth of their colony to relieve themselves outside—and you, too, are relieved. Today, someone is alive in that hive. Tomorrow may be different, for there is still tonight to get through. But for today: that colony is alive.

THE MYTHOLOGY OF beekeeping is that honey bees are magical and mysterious, therefore honey bees are not understood, therefore there is virtually nothing available to learn about honey bees—and therefore one can simply own bees and be amazed by their magic. Beekeeping is easy. It is a reverence that blissfully strolls into ignorance.

It is not enough to simply have bees and care about them. To care about something is to have kind thoughts about it, to worry about it, to feel fondness toward it. These things take place inside one's head and have no effect on the external world. Only actions have effects.

Some people confuse the emotional sense of tenderness or fondness with love. *Love* is a verb. Actions take place in the tangible, physical world. To love something is to behave in a manner that benefits the entity that is loved.

To love is not to care *about* something but rather to care *for* it.

ON A CALM day, plug a stethoscope into your ears and press its bell end against the hive, holding your breath and waiting for the silence between the whoosh of passing cars and the thump of snow clumps falling from the trees. A winter hive sounds like the inside of a large seashell: wind, ghostly whispers, random crackles and tones echoing through the hive entrance. If you are lucky and your listening is well timed, and if there is such a thing to hear, you may observe the quick zap of a bee buzzing its wings or the quiet hum of the clustered colony shifting its position. If you hear such a small and joyous sound, write it down in your beekeeping notes: "On this day, this colony was confirmed alive." Tomorrow may be different, but for today, there is life.

When the winter begins to falter and the days warm toward spring, slide your cellphone inside each hive's entrance and record for a minute or two. Then, press the speaker to your ear with the playback volume at maximum. Hold your breath and listen to the hollow seashell echoes of wind and waves. Listen and hope for the quick buzz or soft hum of living bees.

A hive with the sounds of bees is alive. A hive that is silent may or may not be. The evidence of bees is small and fleeting, so if you do not witness it, you cannot confirm one way or another until spring. Until you can open the hives. Until then, you wait and hold on to hope.

THERE ARE TWO kinds of people who own bees: bee-keepers and bee-havers.

Beehavers *have* bees. They care deeply about their bees. But they haven't researched and learned about how to *keep*, and care for, honey bees. Beehavers observe their hive box with bees flying in and out of it and say their colony is alive. They do not see the spread of disease, the high rate of death, the struggle to survive. The enthusiastic beehaver watches their bees fly to and from the fields and flowering trees, enjoying the opportunity to see the beauty of nature at work.

They may be unaware of the extent of their contribution to the local ecology. Within the walls of their hive, the colony incubates a deadly disorder until it reaches critical mass. As the bees fly about and encounter bees from other hives, they distribute their unwanted gift, a contagious problem that will kill nearly half of the hives it touches.

Other animals such as dogs and cats have also lived for millennia without our interference. So why, when we take one into our possession, do we feed them, give them shelter, protect them from predators and danger, tend to their illnesses and injuries, provide them with medication as needed, and keep a close eye on their health and well-being? Why do we not let our pets and livestock roam freely, find their own food and water, get infested with natural parasites and diseases, and suffer through their injuries and ailments on their own? There are those who do treat their pets this way—perhaps out of ignorance or lack of resources. But if given the information about what an animal needs to thrive and be healthy, as well as the ability and resources to provide such, who with any amount of compassion would allow an animal in their care to suffer? To adopt an animal—be it a cat in the house or a cow in a barn or a colony of honey bees in a hive—is to assume responsibility for their well-being.

Nature is not a perfect pastoral system of gentle harmony and happiness. It is hard, cruel, and destructive of individual beings. To allow a creature within our possession to live without our care and attention is to expose them unnecessarily to hardship, cruelty, and destruction.

Beekeepers, on the other hand, *keep* bees. They *care for* their bees. They know that bee biology and sociology are very different from that of other, more familiar animals. One does not tend to individual bees; one takes care of the needs of the colony as a whole. Relying on intuition and one's knowledge of other species while dealing with the unique needs of bees is foolish.

Beekeepers know that as keepers of bees, they are solely responsible for the bees' entire well-being. A beekeeper is the bees' housing manager, social worker, caterer, and health care provider. And most importantly, the beekeeper is responsible for protecting their bees against the pandemic that has been massacring hives since the late 1900s.

***

WATCH THE THERMOMETER on the porch and the weather reports. When the daytime air warms to a consistent 60 degrees Fahrenheit, and the sun is mild and warm on your face, it is safe to open your hives and inspect.

Gather your beekeeping gear from the cupboard where it has been stored all winter. Your leather gloves are stiff and crumpled but will soften into pliability with the warmth and movement of your fingers. If you were fastidious at the end of the last beekeeping season, your suit will be clean and laundered and spot repaired, and your crowbar-like hive tool will be shiny and clean. If you forgot to check and clean your gear before putting it into winter storage, you will rediscover all the small tears in your suit that need to be patched with duct tape, and your hive tool will stick to your gloved fingers with its lumpy coating of sticky propolis and old wax.

Fire up your smoker. Try to remember the little tricks you have developed over the years to keep it alight.

It has been months, possibly half a year, since you last opened these hives to inspect them. You have not seen the brood chamber, the larvae, the queen, or the colony in its home since last year. You are rusty and nervous, uncertain.

Before opening the first hive, run through your checklist of the basic things you need to have when inspecting a hive. Protective gear. Hive tool. Lit smoker. Clipboard and pencil for taking notes. Hope.

Use both hands to wedge the flat end of your hive tool beneath the hive's lid and pry it loose. The lid resists at first, glued down with the thick, gummy propolis bees make from tree sap and use to seal drafty cracks in the hive walls. With a sharp crack it opens, the propolis stiff and brittle from months of winter cold.

Set aside the lid and the inner lid. Remove the feeder, the moisture-absorbing, padded quilt, the insulating wrap. Pry off any honey boxes that were left in place to feed the bees. Note the weight of each box and compare that to your memory of the weight of a full honey super. Have the bees eaten through all the honey stores and left the box light, or is it still a hefty weight to move, full of food left uneaten by a dead colony?

Does the open hive smell warm and sweet, musty from the long months of being closed—or thick and cold, a pocket of unmoving, uninhabited air?

Note the number of bees on the top of the brood box. Do they rise up and scatter about your fingers in small surprise— or fall unimpeded like tiny dried leaves?

Pry the frames apart gently. Pull the first one out, note its contents of scattered, old food stores, dry rot, alive or dead bees, empty cells. Set it to one side to give you room to pull the other frames.

Even if the hive appears cold and dead, move slowly and gently. There may be a small cluster of bees yet alive somewhere in there.

Pull the next frame, then the next, turning each in your hands like ancient artifacts, searching for clues. What happened? What happened.

TWO PHENOMENA—THROUGH ACCIDENT or design—perpetuate the naive, enthusiastic mindset of beehaving: internet celebrities and gimmicky products.

On social media and video-sharing platforms on the internet, knowledgeable beekeepers post out-of-context videos of themselves working with bees. They move calmly, confidently. *Here is the siding of a house being opened to expose and remove a feral colony of honey bees. Here is a frame of honey being removed for extraction.* The beekeeper may or may not be wearing protective gear. The bees appear calm, unbothered. No one gets stung. Bees are easy to work with, the viewer concludes.

The viewer does not see what has been edited out or not filmed or referenced: the scouting of situation and location; the brutal tools used to cut through honeycomb or wood; the liberal use of smoke to keep the bees calm; and the knowledge and insight the beekeeper used to plan this project, such as analyzing the weather, the season, and the time of day. The factors that influence the beekeeper's movements and decisions are also left out: the shifting pitch of the bees' hum; the speed with which the bees move; and the subtle scents of alarm pheromone, fresh honey, infected larvae. The viewer does not witness the failed attempts, the mistakes, the equipment malfunctions, the stings, the stifled yelps, and the muttered curses.

The viewer sees what is presented to them: beekeeping being done calmly, smoothly, without misadventure. Look how confidently the beekeeper moves, with their bare arms and free-flowing hair. See how cooperative and unconcerned the bees are. This is magic at work: bees and keeper, moving in harmony. Beekeeping is easy.

In advertisements and on store shelves, niche companies offer beekeeping products that promote the idea that beekeeping is an effortless endeavor. Buy this product, fill it with bees, save the ecology, and get delicious honey. Here is an all-in-one beekeeping kit, everything you need in a box: just add a beekeeping suit in your size, and bees! Here is a quirky beehive in an interesting shape or with useful moving parts: just add bees! As though bees were a simple species that just required a box to live in. As though *having bees* and *getting honey* were the only motivations necessary for successful beekeeping.

Thus, the honey bee enthusiast who has not taken an introductory beekeeping course, read a how-to book, or taken another major step in learning about the pastime can be easily swayed into purchasing such deceptively simple and attractive products. They assemble their equipment, purchase a colony of honey bees, and install the bees in their hive. They may have little or no awareness of what to do next, aside from waiting for the right time to harvest honey.

If they don't perform regular colony inspections and take steps to deal with any problems they discover, their hive may develop a myriad of common issues such as parasites, diseases, queen problems, starvation, moisture issues, or overcrowding. Even if they are aware inspections are necessary, if they do not know what they are looking for or how to recognize a problem, inspections become merely an observation of whether bees are in the hive. The mere presence of bees in a hive, however, does not indicate a healthy or thriving colony—it only means that the colony is not dead.

EACH WOODEN, HONEYCOMB-COATED frame you pull is a slice of thin hope. Even if the first few frames are cold and empty, smeared with mold and the feathery trails of invading wax moths, the next frame may be busy with bees, dotted with tiny eggs and plump honey bee larvae.

But you already know which colonies are certainly dead and which hives, if any, have pulled through the winter. You have been watching for months for tiny activity, bees flying in and out of the hive entrances. And you know, as soon as you open the lid of a quiet hive, if the bees are dead. The hollowness is undeniable. The lack of warmth, motion, sweet scent. The opening of the door of an empty house.

What you are looking for, as you pry and pick through empty frames, are answers. What happened? Why are the bees gone?

Catalog the dead. Where are they: all piled on the floor of the hive; clinging to the comb in a desperate cluster; or simply gone, vanished, ghosts? If they are still on the comb, are there food stores right beside them, or are they surrounded by empty cells? What is the ratio of dead bees on the comb to dead bees at the bottom of the hive?

The dead tell stories about the manner of death. Listen carefully for clues. Listen to their silence.

———

THE INTERNET IS full of myths of how non-beekeepers can "help bees." The majority of these tips encourage people to feed the bees, as though honey bees weren't experts on gathering and storing food.

A common myth claims that honey bees who appear tired or listless are lost or hungry. To save tired bees, the advice says, you should set out a dish of something sweet for them to eat: sugar water, honey, crushed hard candies, or grated or mashed fruit.

Yet honey bees are expert navigators that spend their days gathering pollen and nectar and carrying it back to their hives, using visual landmarks, smells, and the sun to find their way. They are unlikely to become disoriented on their familiar routes. And at the end of their short lives, they die away from their hives—in fields, in flowers, on house porches, on roadsides—to save their compatriots the work of disposing of their bodies. Mistaking a dying bee for being tired and lost and giving it something to eat will not help it. An old grandmother who is in palliative care with a failing heart and kidneys and is not expected to live beyond a few days will grow weak and have difficulty staying conscious. If she is given an energy drink or a dose of vitamins, will she gain some energy and open her eyes? Probably. But that effect will be temporary, a few minutes or hours at best, for her body is in the process of shutting down. So, too, will a bee at the end of its life cycle "wake up" and act energized when given a bit of food, but it will then fly off and die anyway.

Ad hoc "bee feeding stations" cause a wealth of problems. Beekeepers do occasionally feed their bees sugar water or sugar syrup but only in certain situations with specific goals: to boost the population of a new or small hive and as supplementary food during off-seasons to ensure the bees do not starve if they run out of honey to eat. Good beekeepers do not set sugar water outside for all manners of bees and pests to access; they use special feeders that are placed inside individual hives so each feeder can only be accessed by bees from that hive.

The idea of foraging bees using a bowl of shredded apples or sugar water as a rest stop during their nectar-gathering day is as illogical as someone carrying home a takeout order from a classy restaurant and stopping en route to eat some cheap fast food. And bees do not understand the concept of a rest stop. If they find food, they simply gather it, take it home, and add it to their food stores.

Sugar water and fruit juice stored by the bees do not magically turn into honey. Honey is made from two ingredients: flower nectar and enzymes from honey bee saliva. The bees offload this mixture into honeycomb inside the hive, then dehydrate it until it thickens into honey. Ripe honey—unlike sugar water or fruit juice—will not ferment or rot, and it can be stored without spoilage indefinitely.

Bees fly up to several miles to forage for food, so any beekeeper within that distance of a "bee feeder" may find their bees have stored sugar water and fruit juice with their honey. Their honey harvest is now ruined.

Tainted honey is a frustrating inconvenience. But the big problem with feeding random bees fruit juice or sugar water takes place right at the feeder itself.

It is rare for more than one bee to be gathering nectar from a flower at the same time, but a larger serving of sweet food can attract dozens or hundreds of bees from multiple hives at once. The community feast distracts them from their natural foraging activities and triggers them into a frantic robbing mode: They follow other bees back to their hives and attack, entire colonies fighting to the death while defending their honey stores. And bees do not know how to keep a polite distance from each other, even when some of them are visibly ill with contagious viruses. And even more contagious and concerning is the transmission of the deadly agent that has devastating effects on the global honey bee population.

A HONEY BEE colony that starved over the winter will still be crowded in its winter cluster, the bees clinging to the honeycomb, a pile of corpses immediately beneath them. They will be surrounded by empty comb cells. There may be food only an inch or two from them. They may have been too cold for the cluster to move and reach it.

A colony that froze will be in its cluster, but with food nearby.

A colony killed by poison—most commonly a sprayed pesticide—will have died quickly, the bees falling to the bottom or in front of the hive, any struggling survivors spasming and twitching.

A colony that suffocated will have their entrances blocked—with ice, an object, or with the bodies of dead bees that piled up too quickly for the hive's undertakers to remove. The inside of the hive will be damp with condensation, and it will smell stale, enclosed, a locked box of stagnant rot.

A colony dead from disease will often have visible signs: bent and twisted wings, visible deformities, wet-looking bodies with a greasy shine.

A colony killed by predators will be obvious: the hive body may be broken open or knocked over and strewn about, equipment and bees scattered like garbage.

A colony that succumbed to parasites will not have been ultimately killed by parasites. It will die instead from starvation, suffocation, or freezing. The population shrinks gradually, the weakened, infected bees dying off and leaving a smaller, more vulnerable colony that continues to dwindle in size. If the piling corpses block the hive entrance, the remaining colony suffocates in the thick, damp air of fermenting honey, rotting bodies, their own tiny breaths.

If the colony becomes too small to create enough warmth to move and access food stores, it will starve. If the colony becomes too small to stay warm during the sudden cold of winter nights, it will freeze. The last few bees die clinging to the honeycomb, a tiny colony huddled together, a massive pile of their deceased sisters beneath them.

UNTIL THE EARLY 2000S, it was relatively rare for an experienced beekeeper to have a notable quantity of their colonies die in the fall or winter. Beekeeping was easy. But now, the average beekeeper loses between a third and a half of their colonies annually. If similar death rates occurred among other livestock—cattle or chickens, for example—it would be considered a global agricultural emergency, and scientists would rush to create a solution. But despite honey bees' critical role in our food production, the public remains largely unaware of the well-documented and singular cause of the steadily increasing mortality of honey bees. No, not poor weather, commercial chemicals, or beekeeper error. The culprit is the varroa mite.

Varroa mites are tiny, multi-legged parasites similar to fleas or ticks. They latch onto honey bees like leeches and feast on their body fluids and fat, weakening them and compromising their immune systems. If honey bees were the size of humans, a varroa mite would be the size of a dinner plate or house cat.

Vigilant beekeepers routinely inspect their hives every few weeks and run periodic tests to check for mites. There is no inoculation or spray that prevents mites from infesting a hive. There are no tiny medicated collars to put around bees' necks to protect them. A beekeeper can only fumigate infected hives or place packets of miticides inside the hives to try to kill the parasites. These treatments take anywhere from an hour to several weeks to administer and have varying rates of success.

If a treatment is successful, the mites die, and the colony is cleaner. For now. But the next time a bee enters the hive, it may bring a parasitic guest. A single pregnant mite that hitchhikes into a beehive on a bee will easily re-infest the entire hive with her quick-breeding, incestuous offspring.

Similar to their cousin the common tick, varroa mites are carriers of multiple viruses that are harmless to humans but contagious and deadly to bees. A colony riddled with mites and mite-borne diseases may survive through the summer, spreading its maladies to all the other hives in the area, but in the cold of fall and winter, it will falter and die. Thus, the origin of the mite's full name: *Varroa destructor.* The destroyer of bees.

CLOSE THE HIVE for protection against rain and scavengers. Later, you will return and disassemble the hive, brush away the dead bees, clean or dispose of the worst frames, set the hardware away in storage. Today, your goal is to do roll call among the colonies, to see who is here, who is gone, and why. What went wrong, what happened. What winter preparation techniques failed horribly, what worked well. What could you have not foreseen. What can you do better.

Open the next hive, and the next. Despite your detailed preparations the year before, some things are simply out of your control. Behind your protective beekeeping hat and veil, you cannot brush away your tears. You are here to work. Grief is not for this moment—it must be set aside and handled later.

Earlier this afternoon, you noticed a bee exiting this next hive. Someone in this hive is alive, and you are looking forward to seeing a live colony, a reprieve from the cold, empty chambers and yet another pile of musty, unmoving bees.

But when you pry off the lid, you are greeted not with the sweet, musty smell of overwintered wax and honey but with a thick, greasy stench. No guard bees fly up to defend their home. The frames are damp and slippery; the comb is glistening instead of matte and dry.

You find the queen. Instead of surrounded by her usual enclave of attendants, she is alone, stepping slowly across the honeycomb with uncertain, jerky movements. On a neighboring frame, a dozen random bees wander as though lost, cold, or mentally incapacitated, moving aimlessly and without purpose. Gag and choke back a cry of disgust and despair. A colony without a queen can possibly be saved—but a sick queen without a warm and nurturing family is helpless, a crying infant abandoned in the woods.

This colony is hopeless. But you must always have hope. Switch out the damp woodware for dry pieces from storage, coax the ailing queen and the few disoriented bees onto the clean, dry comb, and dribble a few drops of last year's honey beside them for emergency food.

It will not work. Within a few days, the queen will also be dead, unable to feed or groom herself without her assistants, or she and her straggling hive citizens will be eaten by spring wasps. There are not enough bees here to defend the hive, to maintain the complex sociological order and processes necessary for colony survival. But you must always have hope. You must always at least try.

SOME BEEKEEPERS RALLY against the use of mite treatments and advocate for the breeding of mite-resistant bees through the process of natural selection. If a beekeeper avoids mite treatments and allows their weaker bees to die off, the logic goes, then only the mite-resistant bees will remain, and they will breed a new generation of hardier bees. While this avenue is being explored by professional bee breeders in strictly controlled settings, when practiced by the individual hobbyist beekeeper, this practice is naive and futile.

In practice, this theory requires a closed system in which select creatures are deliberately bred. If a beekeeper wishes to control their bees' genetics, their queens must be artificially inseminated by males from known stock. Mite-resistant queens that are allowed to mate naturally with random male bees will not result in a pure line of mite-resistant bees; it will result in a line of mixed-breed mutts.

Scientists have their theories, of course, of why the number of mites has skyrocketed in recent years. Of why beekeepers now must be constantly vigilant and take action to keep their mite counts down. Of why the number of hives lost to mites is so high.

Some posit that over the years, the parasites have developed resistance to certain anti-mite treatments, and beekeepers' reliance on these treatments has allowed mites to flourish. Others believe that selective breeding of honey bees for other characteristics has resulted in bees that are genetically weak and unable to defend themselves against mites.

But the use of specific mite treatments is not consistent between countries or even regions. And there are so many different breeds of honey bees—Italian, Buckfast, Carniolan, the list goes on—that it seems unlikely they have all developed the same genetic weakness.

What *is* consistent throughout the developed world is the presence of well-intentioned but misguided beehavers who facilitate the spread of mites and disease by failing to follow best beekeeping practices and thus condemn not only their own hives but all hives in their area.

***

THE NEXT HIVE is empty and cold. And the next. The sunlight is far too mild and pleasant for the occasion. The row of beehives stretches before you like crosses in a graveyard.

Your fingers are cramping from wrenching the hive tool and pulling out stuck frames. Your mind is numb, your eyes dry and burning from tear salt. But you must stay focused, mindful; you must carefully catalog the details, watch for clues. You already know the answers. Every barren frame you pull is just confirmation.

Anger is unscreamed grief. It is a choked-back cry of frustration, dismay. It is a sorrow so deep that it sinks into itself, deeper and deeper, until it implodes, pauses, reverses, and explodes, a sunstar collapsing into itself and sending shockwaves through the solar system.

When you reach the last hive, you rest your hands on its lid and turn your back to the empty, dead colonies. A few bees fly out of this hive's entrance and away. Perhaps they are robbers from other hives in the area, attracted by the scent of honey and wax, seeking easy food. But perhaps, just perhaps, they are residents of this hive, part of a surviving colony. You must always have hope.

MOST HOBBIES ARE not regulated by laws and do not require training. Anyone is permitted to take up gardening, woodwork, singing, or knitting without taking an introductory course. Such hobbies, even if they are done poorly, cannot realistically negatively affect anyone outside of the individual's household and immediate surroundings. There is no need to oversee or regulate such pastimes.

Certain activities, however, pose a risk to the safety and well-being of other beings. Driving a car, for example, flying an ultralight airplane, or shooting targets—such endeavors are overseen by a series of laws, bylaws, and training requirements that ensure proper safety protocol is followed and the risk of outside injury or damage is minimized. The existence, or lack of, laws regarding keeping various animals is also generally influenced by the risks such animals may pose to other people and the ecology if they are mismanaged.

Until the late 1900s, when the varroa mite escaped its origin of Indonesia and began its virus-like spread across the world, honey bees were far easier to keep alive. Since then, not only has the mite spread globally, but beekeeping has also become a trendy hobby adopted by countless well-meaning but underinformed people. Between 1990 and 2020, the number of honey bee colonies in the world increased by nearly 50 percent, from 69 million to over 100 million, many of them owned by enthusiastic yet uneducated beehavers. And mites are now a constant and growing presence on nearly every continent. Most regions are now infested to the point where the parasite can no longer be eradicated, only managed. And the only way to manage varroa mites is for every colony to be thoroughly and regularly inspected and treated for mites.

The standard of allowing people who own bees to self-regulate and (mis)manage their bees, including treating for or ignoring mites as they choose, does not work. This lack of regulation has resulted in the global mite issue becoming critical. Even the most well-intentioned person cannot be expected to follow best practices if they are not aware such guidelines exist. Systems of agricultural regulation, perhaps even standardized licensing systems, must be created and put into practice to ensure that people who own colonies of bees are aware of proper beekeeping practices.

Tragedies don't always happen quickly. Sometimes, they take place slowly. As animals managed by humans, honey bees are unlikely to completely disappear. But the increasing difficulty in keeping colonies alive, and the costs and logistics of replacing those that are lost, is affecting the production and affordability of the food we need to stay alive and healthy. The consequences of having a human population that does not have consistent access to affordable, nutritious food will be wide-ranging and expensive to manage.

PRY OPEN THE lid of the last hive. Hold your breath in anticipation—then breathe deep as you see a soft handful of furry bees moving atop three of the hives' inner frames. The hive air has that now-too-familiar stench of mold and rot—but it is tinged with a sweet, comforting warmth you have not smelled since last fall.

Gratefully, gently, pull and flip and inspect the first few frames. They have the remnants of old honey stores but are otherwise empty, and the wax is dusty with a light coating of mildew. Be unconcerned: you are no longer sleuthing for clues to deaths, and a healthy colony of bees will easily clean up such winter detritus. There is no mystery to solve here. The bees are *alive*.

When you reach the frames occupied by bees, move with more caution, be more present and observant. This colony is quite small, no bigger than your two fists held together. They cannot afford the risk of population damage caused by a dropped frame or an ill-placed fingertip.

With such a small colony, the queen is easy to spot. She appears active and uninjured, moving strategically from comb cell to comb cell on her spidery legs, laying eggs in a precise and steady spiral. It is too early to tell whether her brood is healthy or infected with disease. Only older larvae reveal the symptoms of brood disease, and judging by the number of eggs visible, she only started her spring laying in the past day or two, so it will be at least another week before you can assess the hive's health.

But for now, there is not only hope but also tangible evidence of something to be hopeful for. At the end of a row of boxes of dead and dying bees, there is a tiny, warm, and functioning family of humming honey bees, brood, food, and industriousness spiraling a promising galaxy.

Catch

WHILE TAKING OUT the evening garbage, I see something large glide across the yard and land on the fence by Bill the apple tree. An owl, I assume, given the complete lack of sound. But between the tree branches and the dappled light, I can't really see him.

After several minutes, I tiptoe over to get a better look. Instead of averting my eyes to avoid appearing predatory or hostile, I keep my eyes fixed on him, trying to make out identifying details, knowing well any moment he may spook and fly off.

But instead of startling, the handsome barred owl just turns his head eerily backward and stares at me.

"Hey buddy, whatcha up to, I'd like to pat your feathers." He is within arm's reach, but I don't extend my hand. Despite the urge, I know to respect the space of wild animals. They can carry parasites and disease, and those talons and beak are designed to kill. "Why are you so calm, buddy? Not feeling good, or are you up to something?"

He poses for photos for a few minutes, blinking his inner eyelids up against the flash of my phone. He looks down toward my feet, then back up at me.

I grin, thinking he is deliberately trying to draw my attention to something on the ground. But no, this is not an anthropomorphic cartoon. He likely hears or sees something down there.

I glance down and see it: the live trap we set out to catch the rats. My stomach drops as I realize I haven't checked it in several days. It is sprung, and the rat now trapped inside may have been in there for who knows how long, miserable and hungry in the cold rain. It would be cruel to leave it in there until morning, when B and I would be able to follow our usual procedure of relocating the little prisoners to a local park.

I squat down, adjust the angle of the trap, and glance up at the owl while pointing toward the driveway. "Okay buddy, I'm gonna release him in that direction—do what you want."

I open the trap, and the rat bolts out and down the driveway. Without a whisper of sound, not even a scrape of claws against fence post, the owl lifts his wings and smoothly swoops and grabs. The rat shrieks. Silence.

PART 5

Spring

AS THE WEATHER warms, the quails return to their daily task of egg laying, often so enthusiastically that they produce strange, half-formed eggs or push the eggs out so hard they injure themselves. Dealing with a prolapsed oviduct in poultry is the same as dealing with a prolapsed uterus in cattle. It's like stuffing a duvet back into its cover, only the cover is uncooperative, smelly, and wouldn't respond well if you tried one of those "turn the cover inside out and unroll it over the duvet" hacks.

Rearview Mirror

"THERE'S A BUNNY in the yard," B says.

I am unsurprised. There are always rabbits in the yard: brown cottontails, as lean and lithe as cats, with long, alert ears and ever-twitching noses. They live in the forests behind us, in the piles of equipment by the garage, under the porch, and in the brushes and shrubs and brambles. They come out primarily at dawn and dusk to nibble on the grass and leave their round droppings sprinkled about. When the sun blazes hot and high, they sprawl in the bare dirt at the bases of our apple trees, stretching their limbs and pressing their bellies into the cooler earth. In the winter, they gather under the bird feeders and eat fallen seeds. In the spring, their population increases exponentially, fist-sized babies with tiny, round ears scattering when I approach my garden.

Baby bunnies are always worth mentioning. Or an unusual number of rabbits grazing on the lawn all at once. Or a pair or trio of rabbits doing their delightful chase-and-tag mating dance. But a single rabbit? Not worth talking about.

"There's a bunny in the yard," B repeats.

"Isn't there always?" I reply.

"Not a regular rabbit," he clarifies. "It's a different color than the other rabbits. It looks like someone's pet."

WHILE REFILLING THE bird feeders, I spot a flash of light-colored movement on the far corner of the lawn. A handful of soft brown cottontails is nibbling on the weeds. With them, as distinct and incongruent as a dairy cow among a herd of goats, is a golden-blond bunny with black ears and tail.

Someone's pet, indeed. The coloring of this rabbit is completely unlike a wild rabbit. His fur is the antithesis of camouflage; he will not fare well the next time a hungry coyote comes around.

Keeping my eyes unfocused and averted so as not to appear like a staring, stalking predator, I approach. The cottontails scatter, disappearing into the underbrush of the nearby forest. The blond bunny cocks his ears toward me, a long dandelion leaf disappearing into his mouth, but does not move.

I have had pet rabbits; I know how to handle them, how to move calmly and confidently and pick them up without injury. And I know what to say when approaching a strange cat or dog. But how do I call a rabbit when I don't know its name? Sniffing noises, perhaps? Or do I make the sound of a carrot?

I talk to him softly as I walk in slow circles around him, closer and closer. When I am close enough to touch, I squat beside him. His nose is twitching normally with regular breaths, not flared in alarm or fear, and his alert ears shift to face noises around us. He is entirely unconcerned about my presence.

As he reaches out to bite off another leaf, I stretch my hands over him, intending to grab him by the scruff—but a noisy car drives past on the road out front, passengers hollering and stereo blasting a thumping bass, and the bunny startles, darting into a snarl of blackberries and out of sight.

NIGHTTIME SOUNDS ARE suddenly more relevant, a source of soft anxiety. The crackle of branches under unseen animals' hooves, the querying hoots of owls, the joyous yelps and eerie, alien-like chatter of the coyote pack—these were the soundtrack to a community, an economy, that I was not part of and could only bear witness to. This was a world that went on around me but did not include me. I was like a piece of rock or bit of sunken flotsam in a much bigger and more complex ocean. I could only witness, not move among, these creatures and their lifestyles and interactions.

But now, every rush and crackle of a predator pursuing prey, every plaintive shriek of a rabbit caught by an owl, every celebratory chorus of whoops and howls sung by the hunting coyotes makes me pause and listen, wondering. Is *that* sound the bunny being killed . . . or *that* one?

IN THE EARLY morning, B walks down the driveway to his car, headed for work. The morning rabbits scatter like butterflies from flowers, like grasshoppers from a dusty gravel path. The blond bunny, however, hops alongside him like a loyal dog or attentive child keeping pace with his footsteps.

But B does not have the time to try to catch the bunny, to snare him with his thrown coat, or try to lure him into a pen. B has work to do, a job he must get to. Punch clocks and administrative guidelines leave no room for the organic flow of strange animals, of random rabbits. He gets into his car and navigates carefully down the driveway, as slow as an unfurling leaf, mindfully cautious that there may be a not-very-skittish rabbit under his turning wheels.

As he reaches the end of the driveway and turns onto the road, he glances into the rearview mirror. The blond bunny stands between the tire tracks, ears cocked toward him, one paw lifted from the ground as though about to wave or call out. The bunny grows smaller in his mirror. He turns the corner and is gone.

OVER THE NEXT few weeks, I watch for the bunny, approach him when I can, try to catch him. Although he is not afraid of me, neither is he interested in cooperating. He darts across the road at random, pausing nonchalantly as I try to shoo him back into our yard, frantically looking over my shoulder for incoming cars. He slips under the porch, into bushes, circles around beehives. I follow him onto the property next door, hollering apologies at the wide-eyed neighbors as I trip and flail across their gravely, potholed land. He leads me down the road to an impeccably man-icured lawn lined with No Trespassing signs, then flops down beneath a perfectly pruned shrub. I sit beside the road, catching my breath, chastising him gently. His roaming range is far greater than the hundred-yard-diameter terri-tory generally claimed by the local cottontails. He'd likely hitch a ride into town if he could.

I SHARE BLURRY photos, a brief description of the bunny, and our location to local community groups. I put up signs on newspaper boxes, telephone poles. "Found: Siamese sable domestic rabbit with distinctive markings. Tame but eludes capture."

I receive no calls or messages from any frantic family missing their beloved pet. Instead, an onslaught of care and concern from random strangers, peppered with naive reassurances and condescending laughter.

"There's lots of rabbits here—he's happy where he is."

"I hope the coyotes don't get him."

"A lost-and-found note for a rabbit, give me a break. What next, gonna catch a deer and call it someone's cow?"

"He'll join the local rabbits, and maybe you'll see little different-colored baby bunnies!!"

"It's a damn rabbit, who cares."

But like honey bees and wasps, or sparrows and eagles, domestic European rabbits and western cottontails are not the same species. They have similar behaviors and biology, but they do not naturally interact, and their DNA is so different that they cannot interbreed. A domestic bunny spending time with wild, native rabbits is likely as desperately lonely and bewildered as a mountain goat keeping company with a herd of water buffalo: surrounded by many but having no one to talk to.

Rabbits in the wild have an incredibly short life span: a few months, perhaps a year or two. Every spring through summer, each female produces multiple litters, each consisting of about a half-dozen tiny kits. Hawks, coyotes, owls, and eagles, as well as any domestic cats or dogs that are allowed to roam freely outdoors, feast upon both baby and adult rabbits. By the end of a year, of one female rabbit and her very many offspring, perhaps only one will still be alive. They reproduce at a high rate because they have a high mortality rate: a great number of offspring is necessary to offset the great number of deaths to ensure species survival.

With his anti-camouflage pale fur and wide-ranging territory, the blond bunny is unlikely to survive long. If he is unafraid of people, is he also accustomed to dogs? Would he try to run away from a coyote or assume it was a friend? More weeks than I can count on my fingers have passed since B first caught sight of him. I am surprised he has survived this long.

I NOTE THAT the bunny seems to favor one area of the lawn. It has a patch of dry dirt he likes to lie on and a sprawling bush that provides cool shade during hours of peak heat. I set up our spring-loaded live trap cage next to the patch of dirt, bait it with a handful of birdseed, and lean a large piece of cardboard against it so he isn't tormented by the hot sun if he gets caught while I am away for the afternoon.

I check on the trap hourly throughout the day for a week. Sometimes, it is sprung but empty. Sometimes, it contains an indignant squirrel who yells at me and thrashes about until I release it. Sometimes, the bait seeds have been eaten, but the trap is still set: likely birds, their tiny, nearly weightless bodies too light to set off the spring mechanism. Occasionally, I find the blond bunny sprawled next to the trap, lounging in his little dirt bath, nonchalantly stretching his paws in the sunlight.

ONE MORNING, I see the bunny dozing in the shadow of my quail pen. I consider trapping him in the yard by shutting the gate that surrounds the pen and several of our beehives— but no, the fence has holes in it that the cottontails easily slip through. A fence designed to contain a domestic dog is a poor barrier for keeping out—or in—lithe animals. I retrieve the live trap and set it up a few feet from him with the door open and a handful of birdseed inside. He is unlikely to intentionally enter the trap on his own, but perhaps, just perhaps, as he hops about, he may accidentally walk right into it.

I noodle about the property—tending to my garden, doing small chores—while periodically checking on the bunny. I avoid the area around the quail pen so as not to disturb him, choosing instead to squint at him from a distance.

After several hours of watching him doze, I see he has moved. He is now resting right outside the cage, nose toward its mouth, hindquarters pointed away from it.

I approach him behind, licking my finger and holding it to the air to ensure I am downwind from him. If I sneak up behind him, maybe when he hops away from me, he'll go straight into the cage. Carefully, I squat behind him, hands outstretched. His ears twitch, but he does not move. I touch my fingers to his backside, assuming he'll jump up and forward, but he does not move.

Without pausing to think, I grab his haunches with both hands and shove him forward into the cage. He does not resist. His paws hit the trigger; I jerk my hands back as the trap door snaps shut.

A tiny trap is no home for a rabbit, even for a day or two. B unearths an old wire dog crate from the garage. I furnish it with a water bowl, a pile of lettuce and lawn greens, and a grass-filled box for a litter box. B holds the crate's door open as I prepare to dump the bunny from the trap into the cage, ready to slam it shut should the bunny panic and try to escape. But when I open the trap's door, the bunny just steps forward slowly, bobbing his head up and down and sniffing, then hops into the dog crate. He explores the small space, bobbing and sniffing with alert ears, then sets to nibbling on the head of lettuce.

"This is definitely someone's pet," B says, ruling out the possibility that the bunny may be an escapee from a farm breeding rabbits for meat. "He's probably used to being handled, and the wire cage feels like home."

***

AFTER WEEKS OF searching, I give up on my daydream of reconnecting this creature with a teary-eyed child or heartbroken family missing their beloved pet. No one, apparently, was looking for this animal. No one wanted him returned. I check the calendar for the date on which B first spotted the bunny on our property. It was shortly after Easter.

This beautiful animal, with its friendly demeanor and handsome markings, was likely purchased as a holiday gift. And when the novelty wore off, and the recipient realized that a rabbit is a live animal that needs care they weren't willing or able to give, they abandoned him, jettisoned him like unwanted garbage. I clench my teeth in anger at the sudden realization and imagine the animal's arrival on our property.

At some point, likely in the middle of the night to avoid being seen and questioned, a car stopped near our property. Inside the vehicle was one or more people and a cage or box containing a small, friendly domestic bunny. The bunny had spent its entire life in enclosed spaces: a pen, a barn, or inside a house. Its entire world was created and managed by the people who owned it. It did not know how to survive on its own, to find food or water or safe shelter.

The car door opened. A person emerged, carrying the bunny. The bunny was alarmed by the strange movements and sounds, but it trusted its person.

The person emptied the bunny onto the grass at the side of the road. Suddenly surrounded by unfamiliar scents and sounds, the bunny froze. It did not know where it was, what was happening, or why.

The person got back into the car and drove away. Behind them, illuminated by moonlight, the bunny grew smaller and smaller in their rearview mirror. The car turned the corner and was gone.

Somewhere in the forest, a coyote howled. A wide-eyed owl swiveled its head.

A light rain began to fall.

Another car drove by, startling the bunny.

His fur was getting wet, and he didn't know where home was.

THE PET SHELTERS are full. A shelter volunteer tells me that the number of domestic rabbits that have been recently abandoned by roadsides or rescued from abusive homes is so high that shelters throughout the entire province have closed their doors due to overcrowding. They do not have the room to take in even one small bunny.

I reach out again to community groups, this time expanding my communication to include the local news media and pet shelters. "Found and needing a home: abandoned domestic rabbit of unknown health or history. We cannot keep him. Please contact immediately."

Mindful that people training dogs for illegal dogfighting rings often take advantage of free-pet listings to gather small animals to use as bait, I edit my postings to include a modest adoption fee. I do not intend to collect the money; it is just a deterrent, a filter to sift out the assholes and keep the bunny safe.

My posts and posters again receive a tidal wave of thoughtful-but-naive suggestions and commentary. Several people laughingly accuse me of catching and trying to rehome a wild, native rabbit. A few people offer to adopt him, admitting that they've never had a pet rabbit before but are so taken by his story and beautiful coloring that they'd like to give him a home. And an alarming number of people say we should just release him in one of the many communities of stray and feral rabbits in our region's city parks.

Neither B nor I would consider relinquishing this vulnerable creature to someone who has never previously had or seriously considered having a rabbit. Impulsively and ignorantly adopting an animal that lives for years and needs to be taken care of is exactly why this creature ended up being cruelly abandoned in the first place. B and I want to save this animal, not repeat a cycle that will result in it being further abused and traumatized.

The idea of adding the bunny to one of the many urban colonies of feral rabbits makes my stomach churn with disgust. Doing so would mean we were just as cruel, ignorant, and lazy as the person who'd abandoned him in the first place. And, according to the Criminal Code of Canada 446(1)(b), abandoning a pet is a punishable crime: "Every one commits an offence who... being the owner or the person having the custody or control of a domestic animal... abandons it in distress or willfully neglects or fails to provide suitable and adequate food, water, shelter, and care for it."

Domestic animals left to go "live in the wild" do not enjoy happy, free lives like pastel-colored cartoon creatures in an animated children's movie. They are vulnerable to disease, predators, and injuries, and they incubate and spread viruses and parasites among each other. They may breed and survive a while—but they are vulnerable and likely miserable. Very few domestic pets that get dumped in the wild by their owners end up rescued and taken care of. They generally just die horribly—by disease or exposure, starvation or predators, or injury and infection—after days or weeks or months of confusion and terror.

When domestic cats, rabbits, or dogs are abandoned in feral colonies, they can theoretically be trapped, rehabilitated, and rehomed. But their descendants are truly feral: unaccustomed to human contact and governed by wild instincts and aggressive survival skills. They are also invasive species that cause problems for the native flora and fauna. The best intervention for dealing with feral colonies of domestic animals is to trap and spay or neuter them, release them back into their familiar outdoor homes, and monitor and help them when possible until the colony dwindles and dies off.

B runs his fingers through the fur of one of our cats. She was born into a feral colony, trapped as a kitten, and raised in a shelter until we adopted her. She rolls onto her back and offers up her soft belly for pats as B sighs in resignation.

"I don't want a rabbit. You don't want a rabbit. But it looks like we might have a rabbit."

I CAN SEE hundreds of tiny black creatures wriggling through the bunny's fur. He is infested with fleas, so he has to stay outside, away from our house pets. And I cannot pick him up or pet him for fear of bringing parasites inside the house. I tear a twig from the apple tree and poke it through the bars of the crate, gently brushing the downy fur at the back of his neck. He rests his chin on the ground, and his nose twitches contentedly. When I stop moving the stick, he sits up and bites the stick aggressively. I resume scratching him, and he stretches out, blissed.

Bunnies make delightful pets, but they require as much care as a cat or dog. And we've already got enough creatures to take care of: the bees, the quails, our house pets, our selves, and each other. But if I cannot find someone to adopt him, or a shelter to take him in, we may have to add him to our menagerie.

A dog crate is not suitable housing for a rabbit. They need room to run and play, to explore and stretch their legs. Keeping a cat or dog in a crate for more than a few hours or days would be cruel, and rabbits are basically just vegetarian cats. Our house already has enough indoor animals. B would have to build him an outdoor pen. And B is busy right now with other things, tasks that are more immediately urgent than a lonely bunny that already has food and water and is in a safe place.

I renew my efforts to find the bunny a home, asking friends to help spread the word. I reach out again to the shelters, asking for advice, ideas, resources. And the bunny sits in the dog crate, nibbling on lettuce, or sprawled and dozing.

We get flea treatment, rabbit food, an oversized bale of timothy hay. When I reach into the crate to give him food or water or change his litter box, he watches me with interest, uninterested in escaping. He bumps my hand with his head, asking for pats or tasty treats.

The flea treatment takes several days. When the bunny appears free of crawling parasites, I carefully run my fingers through his fur, bending it backward, looking for injuries, strange marks, other pests. He closes his eyes, nose twitching slowly, and relaxes under my touch. On his haunches I find the thin, dry skin of healing flesh wounds: three hairless scars or skin tears. Perhaps he had a near miss with a hawk or owl. Perhaps he'd been startled and ran into a low fence of barbed wire. Perhaps his previous owners had a dog that attacked him, or a child that played roughly.

A week passes, then another. The bunny has been living in the dog crate for the better part of a month. I do not pick him up and hold him, fearing he may get startled and leap from my arms, and I'd have to catch him all over again. We don't want to keep him, but we're committing to doing so if we have to—and I'm unwilling to risk misplacing an animal we've already spent several hundred dollars on.

In the afternoons, after I give him his daily food, water, and litter box change, I sit next to his crate with the door open and talk to him. I stroke his long, dark ears and the baby-soft fur at the back of his neck and gently scratch his hindquarters. When cottontail rabbits hop past the crate in search of food or a comfortable place to rest, he cocks his ears toward them briefly but otherwise appears uninterested. He nuzzles my hand, nibbles on lettuce, and naps peacefully.

A MESSAGE ARRIVES from a friend of a friend. Unlike other strangers who have contacted me about the bunny, she does not offer pointless platitudes, well-intentioned poor advice, or jeering criticism and ridicule. She has not fallen in love with my photos of the bunny because he is cute and has unique markings. She is not heartbroken by his sad story and impulsively wanting to rescue him.

Her name is Christine, and her pair of house bunnies passed away years ago, and her children have grown up and moved out. Now, she has only a gentle senior cat and lots of space.

We agree to take no action for a few days, to reconsider and think twice, to make plans and gather supplies. One should not adopt a family member in haste.

Two days later, she contacts me again. She has a litter box, food, and a large pen for him to live in while he acclimatizes to her house. Are we still looking for someone to adopt the bunny, she asks, and if so, when and where can we meet up?

AT THE END of the hour-long drive, we open the back door of our vehicle to unload our small passenger and the bags of hay and rabbit food. The bunny is shaking with terror. He cowers at the back of the cat carrier, eyes wide and nostrils flared with panicked breaths. The last time he was in a car, the last time he was shaken by the grumbling vibration of road beneath wheels and smelled the close-up stench of gasoline and exhaust, was when he was driven to our property and abandoned into fear and loneliness.

Christine welcomes us with a warm smile and a whistling kettle. Her cat flits around her feet and disappears into another room. A large pen furnished with litter box, food, water, and an empty cardboard box occupies most of her living room. I set the cat carrier inside the pen and open its door so the bunny can recover from his travels. If he doesn't exit the carrier on his own, I may have to lift it and dump him out. But at least he can get used to the new smells and surroundings first.

We sit down to tea, cookies, and a bowl of fresh cherries. After twenty minutes of conversation, I realize I have forgotten about the bunny—I excuse myself to the living room to reassure him with my smell and presence that he has not been abandoned again.

The bunny, however, is unconcerned. He is busy thoroughly sniffing all corners of the pen, standing on his hind legs and bobbing his head to see the furniture beyond. His ears are tall and alert, his eyes bright. He has used the litter box and messily rummaged through his pile of food. I retrieve the empty cat carrier.

Back at the table, I report my findings. Christine smiles warmly. B looks relieved. Christine tells us she is naming him Frodo, after J. R. R. Tolkien's character and in homage to his long journey and unknown adventures.

We gather our things to leave, and I lean into the pen to give Frodo a last pat and say goodbye. But he is playing with his cardboard box, chewing on its flaps and pushing it around with his head. He has had enough of me and is too busy with Important Bunny Things to be bothered to bid farewell.

As we pull out of the driveway and start down the road, I glance in the rearview mirror. Christine is standing at her living room window, waving and smiling, her cat cradled in an arm. Behind her, out of sight, a Siamese sable rabbit named Frodo cheerfully destroys a cardboard box.

Christine grows smaller and smaller in the rearview mirror until she becomes a pale dot framed by a window-pane framed by the mirror. We turn the corner and are gone.

Housewarming

The crow feeder is empty, again. It never stays full for long.

Sometimes, we put small, shiny trinkets—metal washers and bolts, crumpled bits of tinfoil—in the crow feeder, but the birds never take them. They only take the food: peanuts, a big bowl of peanuts twice a day, sometimes eggs from my quails or a handful of stale pastries. Crows allegedly like shiny things, but apparently, we haven't offered them the right kind of shiny things.

I have heard stories of crows bringing gifts—small rocks or bits of colorful plastic left beside a bird feeder or on a windowsill—to those who feed them. But all we've ever found left near the crow feeder has been crushed peanut shells and our ignored metal offerings. Perhaps we're not worthy of gifts. Or perhaps we're too stupid and ignorant to recognize such things, kicking aside a pretty pebble on the doorstep or trampling an elastic band beneath our clumsy feet.

I dump peanuts into the feeder, burying the random rejected gifts, and hear a crow, high in the trees and invisible to me, call out. There is always a sentry posted. I turn and walk back to the house. Behind me, the ethereal sound of a dozen or more pairs of wings swooping down and landing on the fence alongside the feeder.

From a chair on the porch, I watch the crows enjoying their snack. They're remarkably polite and organized. Each bird steps into the feeder, grabs a nut or two, then flies off, making room for the next crow. The trees are a cacophony of wings and caws as the birds swoop from feeder to tree and back.

The crow feeder empties over several minutes. The flying birds lessen, and the air quiets. A few remain around the feeder, searching the ground for leftovers and dropped nuts. Soon, the flock will depart.

Today, though, they do not leave so quickly.

One crow lands in the middle of the lawn, a few yards from the feeder. He is carrying something in his beak. He sets it down on the ground and caws, bobbing his head.

A handful of crows glide down from the trees and form a loose circle around the object. They caw at it, stretching their necks toward it and bowing theatrically. After a good minute of noisy proclamation, they all fly back into the trees.

Cautiously, I step off the porch and approach, keeping my eyes affixed on the item they were so enthusiastic about.

It is a stick.

I pick it up and examine it. It is nearly two feet long, the diameter of my smallest finger, smooth and free of splintering cracks or bumpy leaf buds, with a slight bend toward one end. I walk back to the porch, holding up the stick and admiring it. It is a fine stick, a very good stick, for our nest.

As I open the door and step inside, I hear behind me an uplift of wings, the rhythmic wind of dozens of birds leaving the trees.

Once Upon a Holly Tree

FRIENDS ENVY THEIR pastoral lifestyle. They call her Snow White, a rural damsel surrounded by rabbits, deer, and crooked trees bearing red fruit. Snow White and the prince, happily ever after.

In summer afternoons while the prince is at work, she finds another dead rabbit in the garden, its soft body stiff and twisted from a neighbor's rat poison. A curious audience of deer gather in the backyard, dark eyes and down-filled ears turned toward her as she scoops the small body with a shovel, avoiding the fleas and ticks that might be seeking warmer blood, and moves it to a forest grove for the night-time scavengers to address.

PERHAPS THIS IS the afterlife. Or, more appropriately, the afterdeath.

ONCE UPON A time she was a teenaged girl, as sad and dark as she was quiet. She lived in a small town surrounded by few friends and many people who said ugly words to her, and she felt alone. She fell down a lot. She always felt like she was falling. She wrote dark poetry, listened to angry songs on repeat, and collected sharp objects and reasons to die, or leave, or simply not exist.

On a bright spring day, a friend drove her to a party. The car engine squealed, the wheels skidded, and everything was blood and broken. The falling dark girl fell further into darkness. No happily ever after.

But a few days later—the blip of a heart monitor. A blink into consciousness. Here. Now.

And the years turned by. And the falling dark girl fell no further into the darkness.

But she knew that Death stayed close: every footstep across a busy intersection could meet a speeding car; every swallow of food could clog a trachea; every step up a ladder could slip and sever a spine. And she knows all the spells to conjure Death: the razors, hoarded pills, knives, poisons. The high places with hard landings. The dark, deep water of the lake. She leaves her notebook closed, does not read her old writings. The last pages are yet blank, the last sentence unfinished, ending in a semicolon.

There is no happily ever after. But there is an after—this time. This is not always so.

AT FORTY-SEVEN, THE prince slipped sideways from consciousness into some other world characterized by bright lights, familiar faces, and strange conversations with those long gone. He woke up in a bed surrounded by tubes and wires, his face smashed by the sudden collapse, ribs cracked and back bruised from aggressive CPR pounded into his chest.

There is no memory of death itself. Only that of before and after. Between, there are dreams, stories written by angels, myths, oxygen-deprived brains.

***

YOU MAY HAVE been there, so close to death it can only be described in metaphor. You have leaned across or been pushed through that dark doorway, that black maw. You've felt the stench of hot breath rushing up into your face, felt your fingers curl around the edges—and you are here, with the long stare and quiet of those who have traveled a long distance alone.

We can only describe the journey back if we know where we've been.

***

HEALING IS NOT a reversal of damage, a negation of what has happened. It is not a backward movement. It is a movement forward.

In their backyard, there is a holly tree that was broken in a windstorm. Its trunk had cracked, split, and the tree fell over; its top branches came to rest pressed atop a small grove of pines. The holly tree survived—the cracked and broken trunk oozed sap, grew new wood and bark, and closed. The tree grew new waxy, spiky green leaves, and each spring, it starts a new crop of red berries. The tree is healed and healthy. But its top still rests against the grove of pines. In healing, the tree did not reverse its fall, pull itself back upright. It is healed and healthy, but it will never be the same.

The human body has an incredible capacity for recovering from wounds and growing new tissue. But it does not rearrange the cells; it grows new ones. The ends of a broken bone will generate new bone tissue, cover the distance between the pieces, and heal. But the body cannot pull misaligned bone fragments back into their original positions—they heal where they are: crooked, lopsided, misaligned. And that change in position, be it ever so slight, will affect the body's kinetic dynamics: how the muscles move, the angle of the joints, how the nerves and tissues configure themselves.

So, too, for the flow of blood through severed veins, the electric spark of neurons across frayed spinal cords, the flex and thud of torn muscle and heart tissue. We will never be the same.

———

IN AUTUMN, SHE collects seeds from her flowers to save for the winter birds, as she has done since childhood. In the parched, dry summer, he digs a hole, lays a waterline so the night animals can drink. She brews thick syrup for the hummingbirds in winter, thin syrup in summer. He builds houses for birds and bats and rearranges his workshop renovation plans to accommodate the nests he finds in the rafters.

Some say they should build a fence to keep the rabbits and deer from her garden, but she shakes her head. She does not mind the nibbled leaves, the torn-up roots, the heart-shaped hoofprints that punctuate her soil. She is amused by the tiny pawprints, the quiet eyes that watch from the grass, pretending to be invisible.

In spring, she picks tiny carcasses from the melting snow, arranges their bones to weather and dry. He lifts lids from beehives, breathes in the scent of warm wax or cold, musty death. Hawks turn above, hunting tiny rabbits and quick-darting mice.

———

FIREMAN. MAN OF fire. A man who seeks fire, is created and shaped by fire, is broken by fire.

An acquaintance overhears the name of their rural hometown, laughs, comments that the prince must have a pretty quiet job because there's not many buildings to catch fire. But when old ladies' hearts seize, a gas leak sputters awake, the highway bridge cracks and falls and tosses cars like pebbles, airplanes crash into buildings, the firefighters arrive first. Who else has towering ladders, heavy hydraulic tools, jaws of life, and layers of muscle and sinew tensed for action and trained in navigating destroyed buildings and hauling deadweight bodies. Who else can free the crumpled children from car wrecks or the buried bodies from broken buildings, so the paramedics can wrap them with bandages and splints, the police with handcuffs and paperwork, or the coroner with resolution and body bags.

Who else can choose to bear the weight of moments that leave the mind twisted and broken. The rasping breath of a crushed and dying body. The scream of a child calling for his mother. How much violence can a body endure and still survive. How much grief can a mind carry and still awaken in the morning, fill out paperwork, brew coffee. A hand slammed on a counter in frustration. A back bent, jaw clenched with the shudder of unspoken rage.

When Timmy falls down the well, you picture a bright-red cartoon firetruck racing to the rescue. It is not the whole truth, but it is truth enough.

FRIENDS ASK HER, *How has your life changed since the accident?* And she cannot answer. She does not know how to compare the life she has with the one that does not exist. And it has been so many years now.

Is this the afterlife, or a dream, perhaps. This strange and fascinating world characterized by the surreal brightness of colors, the delightful déjà vu of small, familiar things. Fresh water tastes like the smell of wet dog, clocks' hands seem to turn backward, and sunshine on her face feels deliciously fresh. She wonders how to distinguish between the shift in perception and attitude caused by the brush with death and the shift in cognition caused by the brain injury. And does it really matter.

Or perhaps she was sleeping and is now awake, trying to reconcile her experiences with fading dreams. The moment of confusion when a dream is recounted as fact: "Don't you remember? We spoke just yesterday."

After returning from a long journey to a strange land, one's home seems familiar but odd; well-wandered streets seem stilted and bright, as though from a movie. The process of reconnecting is a disconnect. A long stare, remembering.

WHEN SNOW WHITE and the prince part ways, even briefly, they always share an embrace and an *I love you*. They have both been there and returned. And they have seen those who did not. Next time, they might not.

The boy whose heart seized suddenly during soccer practice. The man whose tractor tipped, crushing him in a distant field. The woman who slept through a gas leak, dreams slipping into deeper dreams. The man who went walking at night, darted into the road to pull his dog back from a speeding truck—his shoe left lonely by the road as the ambulance sped pointlessly away. His wife recounts their last conversation, sharp and bitter as frozen mud.

These could be your last words. What will they be. The slammed door. Anything could be the last thing you say to her. "I'm going to the store; back in five. I love you."

TOUCHING DEATH IS not like going on a journey and returning home to the same place. It is stepping out of a room and entering a confusing and many-angled hallway, then walking through another door into a room that looks familiar. Is it the same room from a different angle? Or another room that looks similar?

Trying to decipher the truth is like comparing two pictures in a child's magazine—something is different, but what. The furniture has been rearranged, the walls repainted, but is it the same room.

THEY CALL HIM *hero*. They praise him for his bravery, for saving lives. But after decades of hauling bodies from burning buildings, breathing air into smoke-clogged lungs, palming tourniquets against severed limbs and pulsing wounds, he cannot claim to have saved a single life. The patient is loaded onto a stretcher, the ambulance lights flash, the sirens scream away—and the firefighters are left to pick up hoses, wash blood from the pavement, fill out forms for an incident for which they will never know the outcome.

WHILE PICKING BLACKBERRIES on a sun-bleached afternoon, she realizes she forgot to check the rat traps. Every morning, she empties the hand-sized traps tied to the fence and disposes of the dead as needed. But not this morning.

The rat is standing up like a little bright-eyed man, one front paw resting on the closed jaw of the black trap, the other folded softly as though about to reach out and open. Beneath it, its hind leg is twisted at too many angles. The rat stares at her with round, dark eyes. She is touched by the curve of its tail draped softly over the fence's bottom wire. She is sorry for the heavy, dry heat, her negligence, the hours of struggle and pain.

She calls out to the prince. They speak a moment. Their eyes are guarded with the echoes of a restless night of aching bones, broken sleep, muttered disagreements, a morning marred by short-tempered words. She returns to her garden.

She glances over her shoulder and sees him walking toward the rat with a heavy fence post balanced on his shoulder. His muscles flex. His face is solemn, his head bowed. She turns her back, picks blackberries.

Thump.

LIKE BIRTH, DEATH is rarely quick, elegant, or silent. When the family members ask, he always tells them their beloved went instantly, knew no pain, did not suffer. Why would he say anything else.

Suicides. Heart attacks. Car accidents. Death slips into his workdays like unscheduled meetings that brush aside schedules, plans, commitments. The pager goes off at noon, dinnertime, 3:00 AM, and it's work gear on sirens screaming engines steaming down roads clotted with ice cars bodies to save lives pronounce death witness the struggle between one and the next.

In a fairy tale, death would come quiet and easy. It would always be welcomed or deserved. It would be given, and received, as a gift or a long-awaited resolution.

AS THE PRINCE sleeps, she keeps one hand on him, or a quiet, outstretched foot. When she wakes, she feels his warmth, pauses, and listens for the quiet hush of breath. Mothers of young children do the same. *Are you alive, are you alive.*

She turns off the stove, adds lids to the pots. When he is late from work, he usually calls, sends a message. Her hand shakes as she pours another cup of tea. He knows a delayed dinner or a shift in evening plans is but a mere inconvenience; it is reassurance he needs to urgently convey. *I'm alive, I'm alive. At this moment, I am alive.* She turns her back to the clock, busies herself with small, inconsequential tasks, tries not to hold her breath to better hear the crunch of tires on the gravel driveway. *Are you alive, are you alive. At this moment, are you alive.*

WE ARGUE ABOUT when life begins and ends. As though it were binary, a light switch. Is the heart beating. Are the nerves responding. Is there brain activity. But what we are afraid of is not muscle or neurons but consciousness—or the lack of it. We do not fear the body dying so much as that of the mind surviving. We fear nightmares, a conscious mind trapped in an unresponsive body; we shudder at tales of anesthetized patients frozen and awake under the surgeon's knife, theories of autopsied cadavers sensing the sharpness of the coroner's scalpel.

We ask those who have touched death, *What do you remember?* And we expect tales of some strange land, as though they had taken a journey. Their scars and mending bones are souvenirs that tell truncated and unsatisfying stories.

HE THRASHES IN dreams, yells out, caught in the half-world of those he has seen crushed, mauled, tangled in the tentacles of disfiguration and death. She tries to wake him, pull him back. Sometimes, she cannot. There are those who watch the dying. And there are those who watch the watchers.

In the mornings, they snarl and pace like restless monsters, fanged beasts conjured by broken sleep and the anxious uncertainty of aging scar tissue. She squints through the blinding scotoma of seizures and migraines; he limps through the gauntlet of old injuries. He tries not to yell. She tries not to leave. They cling to each other with clawed hands, hissing and crying quietly, struggling to not drown in their own shadows. There are those who tame the monsters. And there are those who try not to become them.

———

TOUCHING ONE'S OWN death does not leave one unscarred or unbroken. Death works in tandem with a sidekick named Trauma. Trauma carries two weapons: one to break bodies and one to break minds.

Death touches the dying. Trauma touches all: those who survive and those who bear witness.

He brings back stories from the siren-filled battlefields of first responder frontlines. Respectful of Trauma's reach, he chooses his words carefully, avoids adjectives when describing victims. She suggests vague descriptors: *insides on the outside, bits and pieces, crispy chicken.*

For them, injuries and fatalities are not pictures on a computer screen, news reports to be ogled and discussed like staged reality show entertainment. Death and Trauma are as real as the scars on their hands, the blood in the toilet bowl—and they are cautious not to look too closely.

———

HER FRIEND MISQUOTES doctors and insists that once healed, the body returns to a stable normality, and all injury is reversed. Two years, the friend says, the body continues to heal for up to two years. After that, it's done.

The arthritic bone spur in her neck grates as she shakes her head in disagreement. She thinks of the medicine cabinet filled with painkillers and herbal remedies, remembers years of ongoing chiropractic therapy and neurology tests.

She holds her face calm against the urge to grind her teeth and shriek, to tear at her hair and fling claws of fury against the skies. How to explain. How to describe the endless, desperate search for relief from a body that betrays her, that falls apart in odd and unexpected ways. The experiments with magnets, heat, or strange ritualistic stretches. The daydreams of smashing aching bones with a hammer to ease the swelling pain. The nightmare of waking into unresponsive limbs cold and heavy with the sharp ache of neuralgia. The nightmare of a glass-coffin body that cracks and stabs her with shards as she lies within it, screaming silently.

She leans to one side to ease pressure off a nerve pinched in her twisted back and mentions the holly tree.

HE COUNTS THE deer on his bent, heavily scarred fingers. The dark fungus of arthritis in his knuckles keeps him awake at night. In the mornings, the deer watch him from beneath the apple trees with big eyes and soft, attentive ears, stepping elegantly through the weeds like stilettoed dancers.

He counts the deer, compares the number to memory. Is anyone missing. Are there more. The wild-eyed doe who leapt from the shadows, too close as headlights flashed her flank, a screeching thump, then a staggering limp into the forest. Each time the buck steps into the forest on his annual migration route, the prince hopes he'll return, never knowing until he does, never certain.

SHE STANDS BY the holly tree, raises her lily-white hands to the clear-blue sky, and sings, picturing a candy-red firetruck passing by with smiling firefighters leaning out the windows, waving. The birds do not land on her and twitter in harmony; the forest creatures do not gather at her feet. Her back is crooked with mishealed broken bones; his neck is bent with the weight of memories. They are holly trees, reincarnated.

She carries quiet ghosts, is haunted. The prince carries a gun. Their bones chatter and creak with the aching language of the undead otherworld. They wrap their arms around each other and look long into the sunset, drink fresh, clear water, watch for the deer. There is no happily ever after. This is the after.

Fledge

GARDENING. I STAND up, brush the dirt from my knees, and there on the fence post, not two feet from my face, is perched a young swallow. Just yesterday, I'd been tiptoeing around the birdhouse with my camera, photographing the trio of young birds as they jostled for position in the birdhouse door, as their parents swooped and soared and brought them flies and bees, sweet treats for teenaged birds. I recognize the fluffy white breast, the remnants of rubbery-yellow baby-bird lips. Newly fledged, the chick is likely experiencing their first day away from the nest.

The young bird cocks their head at me, blinks, produces the tiniest *cheep.* There is so much wildlife on our property that I've trained myself to not flinch or jump lest I startle anyone, so when the bird bows their head a little and starts to open their wings, I do not move but instinctively squeeze my eyes shut. A flutter of wings through the air toward me, click of tiny claws close to my face, soft brush of feathers against my cheek as they try to perch on the frame of my glasses. I breathe softly, amazed at the lack of weight. *What must this look like*, I think. *My body, head, and hair—but in lieu of a face, the bright white and iridescent bluegreen of a small but elegant bird.*

Then, they are gone. I open my eyes; the bird is back on the fence, looking at me. They open their wings a bit, I squeeze my eyes shut—a small rush of air toward me, tiny feet on the side of my head, scrabbling for purchase in my hair, feathers brushing against my ear and forehead.

Then, gone again. I open my eyes. This time, the bird barely pauses on the fence. They land, turn, and fly toward me again. This time, I will myself to keep my eyes open. Tiny feet atop my head. A blur of feathers at the edge of my vision. The bird slips and dances, trying to find a foothold. *Balance,* I think. *Balance.*

Then, gone again, a swooping arc away from me, landing farther down the fence, beyond the sunflowers, looking back at me with tiny, bright eyes, soft and weightless in the warm afternoon light, a life so new and naively trusting I could count it in days, cup it in my two hands.

Exodus

TO SEE CLEARLY, stand back.

A tree's branches will match the arrangement of its roots.

When things fall apart, or undergo a radical or systemic change, one must zoom out to see the new patterns among the chaos.

Go back to the roots. Dig deep into the dust, the past. Then, turn around. Look back, then up.

I WAIT BY the car as B checks the house one last time before we head out. Is the stove off? Are the windows closed? Is the toilet lid up in case the pet sitter is delayed and the pets' water bowls run dry?

A few days' vacation away from our little homestead to visit friends in another town is needed and appreciated but preceded by much preparation and anxious double-checking of details. I distract myself from my worries by thinking instead of who and what I look forward to seeing during the long drive and at our destination. Our friends, certainly, and their menageries of children and pets. Perhaps we will catch sight of random animals along the highway: deer, eagles, dopey-eyed dairy cows, a herd of mountain goats. Perhaps I will see the horses.

RUNALONGS ARE THE tireless companions of a passenger on a long drive through the countryside. Most often seen by bored and imaginative children who lean their heads against the window and stare out at the passing scenery, they are creatures or figures that run or fly alongside the road, keeping pace with the vehicle, leaping from fence post to fence post or galloping through the trees. Dogs and large cats are common, as are mystical beings such as giant birds, long-limbed humanoids, or characters from video games or movies. They are rarely malicious but often intimidating. They tend to disappear when the car slows or stops, or when the road enters an urbanized area of buildings and walls. Perhaps they are there to protect or amuse. Perhaps they simply like to run.

My runalongs were horses: big chestnut steeds with thick, curved muscles and shining coats. There was rarely just one but never so many as a herd. They galloped ahead of or alongside the car in the gravel and grass beside the road, and when the car slowed for a crossroad or stopped for a passing train, they'd veer off out of sight into the trees or over a hill, then reappear a few miles later, thundering out of a forest and downhill in an avalanche of manes and hooves.

I still find them in my dreams, my runalong horses, huge and powerful creatures. Most often they are swimming or wading across a dark lake or river, or standing on its shore, head high and alert. They will carry you across, if you need, though their alliances and temperament are unknown. They always know the way, and they never make eye contact.

TASKS TO BE DONE BEFORE A VACATION:

- mow lawn

- ensure garden soaker hose is working well

- weed garden

- harvest and give away any ripening produce in the garden or on the trees

- clean quail cage and refill dust bath with fresh sand

- thoroughly check all the beehives

- attend to any problems in the beehives

- add honey boxes to hives that may get crowded while we are gone

- fill bird feeders

- clean and refill hummingbird feeders

- water potted plants

- refill wasp traps

- remove rat traps

- stock up on pet food

- ask neighbor or friend to take care of pets and check the mail

- toss any aging food from the fridge

- take out garbage

- pack

ONCE UPON A time, this land was covered in ice. As the climate warmed, glaciers melted free from the mountaintops and slipped downward, toward the ocean, slowly skidding hundreds of miles across the land, dragging rocks and leaving huge, flat-topped moraine piles of glacial till alongside their paths, long river tails trailing in their wake.

The people came, following the glacier-gouged valley rivers like crowds of ants, digging into the gravelly soil and building structures and infrastructure, threadlike highways and spiderwebbings of secondary roads.

When their homes become crowded, ants, like honey bees, send out scouts to seek potential new locations. They leave and return, then leave and return again, until a location is found and the colony leaves for good.

A small forest animal moves into an abandoned den. A swarm of honey bees takes over an empty hive. A mason bee nests in the holes left behind by wood-burrowing insects. Humans, like animals, migrate away from what harms them or holds them down and toward that which serves them well. And that which they leave behind is taken over by others.

AN URBAN DWELLER without pets or plants can leave their home relatively easily. Toss any aging food from the fridge, take out the garbage, pack the luggage, lock the door. Barring any unforeseen emergencies such as a burst pipe or robbery, most urban dwellings can be left unoccupied for long stretches without consequence. Only physical possessions, trinkets and clothing and appliances, are being left alone.

But many rural dwellers cannot step away from their homes so easily. Someone must be left to take care of the plants and animals in their absence. Even then, there's only so much one can expect a friend or neighbor to do, even for a thankful wage.

When we leave our homestead, our house pets need to be fed and attended to, certainly. And the quails must be given water and food—but their eggs can be left ungathered, and their dust bath can remain unfilled for a few days. The garden can grow weeds, though its produce is free for the picking. The lawn can be left unmowed. And the rows of beehives can be largely ignored, though the phone number of another local beekeeper should be left in case of emergency. The bees and the birds and the plants will be fine, or they won't. There is only so much that can be done while we are gone. And we will not be gone long, for this is our home, and our charges need us as much as we need them.

A SINGLE HONEY bee cannot survive on its own, any more than an engine can travel without being attached to a car or a heart can beat without its body. A honey bee colony is a superorganism. Within the colony, groups of bees take on individual tasks: gathering food, protecting, reproducing, building housing. No one bee can do all this work at once, and yet it is all necessary for survival.

Like any other animals, colonies of bees will abandon a home that is under threat and relocate to a region with more favorable conditions. They may flee due to sudden catastrophe such as forest fire or volcano or landslide—or they may gradually shift their location in response to slower processes such as climate change or urban development. And they will not go far: only as far as they need to find suitable homes and resources that fill their needs.

Human beings, who are also animals, sometimes have to relocate for financial and psychological survival. To stay in one place and resist change is death. But we must also maintain or rebuild our colony, for we are hive animals and cannot survive on our own.

TYPICALLY, WHEN SOMEONE lives in an apartment or townhouse, their community, connections, and responsibilities exist beyond the walls of their home, out in the world. Aside from perhaps a few small pets and houseplants, and biodegradable food and garbage, the contents of such a dwelling can generally be left for weeks or even years and they will remain in stasis, unchanged.

But a rural farm or acreage is a micro-community unto itself, a spread of land inhabited by flora and fauna both wild and domestic. Like the managers of a complex business, we may step away from our home-based responsibilities for a few days or longer, but doing so requires that we pre-emptively attend to our chores before leaving, assign tasks to an assistant, and be prepared for things to go awry and for there to be more work to be done when we return. The garden may fester into aphids and weeds and blight. The blackberry bushes on the edge of the forest may sprout angry octopus arms of thorn-covered tendrils across our lawn. The bees may swarm or be attacked by colonies of wasps. There may be death. There may be chaos.

Or everything may be fine. The lawn may be a bit long, and the garden may sprout a few weeds among a lush crop of produce. The house pets will be excited and confused at our return. The quails will not have noticed our absence; their food tray will be overfilled and their pen accessorized with tiny eggs I can gift to the crows. The beehives will be calm and healthy, robust and filling with honey.

I STAND BY the luggage-filled car, waiting for B to join me, and stare off in the direction of the ocean. It is far beyond the fields and corner stores of our little town, past the visible horizon, an hour and many miles away—but I know that in a week or two, there will be a storm brewing above it, a great fist of wind and fury that will snap power lines and send lawn furniture spinning and wild animals scurrying for shelter. The storm will likely reach here, but not this week, not today. It takes time for such waves to roll across the landscape. Today, the air is calm, scented with cow manure and fresh-cut grass and the dust of industrial de(con)struction, with the faint red glow of the metropolis on the western horizon. Unravelation: a calm moment of insight among upheaval and chaos.

One day, we will leave our little acreage for the last time, all our possessions packed or strapped in a truck, and we will drive away toward some new home. I picture it like a scene from a hillbilly comedy or a cartoon: the quails in their cage strapped to the roof, beehives tilting out the back, a grafted branch from Bill the apple tree poking out the window. As we drive down the road and turn the corner, we will see, gathered on the lawn, the rabbits and deer and rats and coyotes and crows and raptors watching us as we go. They will wait for our return, but they will hear only the sharp smack of surveyor's stakes being driven into the ground, the hollow echoes of an empty house and workshop, and the grumble of approaching bulldozers.

Or perhaps they will follow us, a mélange of runalongs: the hummingbirds and finches clinging to bird feeders strung from the truck's antenna, the rats and rabbits leaping and scrambling to hide among our furniture and boxes, the deer and coyote loping alongside us. As B drives and I doze and dream down the road past the township's limits, down the highway, through the mountains and valleys and fields and small towns, beyond the shadow of the looming tsunami wave of the spreading metropolis, the animals will disappear, veering off into the untouched forests and scattering throughout the farmyards and barns like wild horses.

I still find them in my dreams sometimes. My runalong horses. They stand on the shores of a dark lake, a night sky with or without explosions overhead. If I approach them gently and confidently, they will let me ride them as they swim across the dark water, embers falling around us, to whatever unknown forest is on the other side. Perhaps they will accompany us on this trip. Perhaps they will lead us when we leave for good.

You can only stand so tall when you have to stoop and curve to fit within an ever-crowding environment, to survive on shrinking resources. A young tree in a terra-cotta pot will be stunted, bonsaied if its roots cannot reach and spread. Sometimes, you have to leave and drive away to find suitable space. A migration of one household. Window down, elbow in the slipstream breeze, sunlight a soft hand on the shoulder, good music on the speakers. Crank it up, crank it out, gas pedal sinking to the floor, long-winged birds flying. Surviving becomes thriving when transplanted to appropriate soil.

The past does not change. The roots of a tree remain stable even when the trunk is broken. Although everything else may alter and shift, our roots hold us up, help us grow. Dead bees still sting, though they don't make much honey, and the surviving colony splits and flies away in a swarm, splits again and flies away. The migrating animals veer farther east or north, away from the waves of industry and development. Cycles shift in response to the systemic change. And its flavors may change, but there will always be honey somewhere, and there will always be someone who gets stung.

A Rural Lexicon

ASTRONAUT SUIT: a specialized set of protective white coveralls worn by a beekeeper

BEEHAVER: *bee* + the verb *to have*. A person who possesses one or more colonies of bees but does not do the hands-on work of taking care of them—as compared to a bee*keeper*, a person who possesses bees and diligently monitors them and attends to their ailments and problems

BEEMERGENCY: any urgent situation involving bees

BEESPLAINING: the phenomenon of a non-beekeeper confidently and erroneously explaining the intricacies of honey bees and beekeeping to an experienced beekeeper

BLUE-TIPPED PRICKLEPINES, EASYCARE PRETTYBUSHES, NEEDLESHEDDING FLAKEBARKS, and **POLLENBOMB SAPDRIPPERS:** various trees and shrubs as spoken of by someone who is quite ignorant of silviculture

BORING BROWN BIRDS: small, seed-eating, sparrowlike birds of any color

BOX OF BEES: a technically alive but doomed-to-fail colony of honey bees that is beyond hope of rescuing

BUN or **FUZZYBUTT**: a wild cottontail rabbit. The younger and smaller the animal is, the more syllables are used in reference to it: e.g., a fist-sized, three-week-old kit is a bunbunbun

BUNNY BUCKET or **BUNNY TROUGH**: a shallow bin or trough with a hose running into it, for the purpose of providing water to wildlife during a drought

BUZZTARD: *buzz* + *bastard*. A wasp or hornet

CROW GUNS: large, clacking, bird-deterrent noisemakers placed in fields and orchards

CROW O'CLOCK: the hour before dusk when the estimated ten thousand crows that scavenge for food in Metro Vancouver, Canada, fly en masse over the communities east of Vancouver to their evening nesting sites, often appearing to fly out of the sunset

CRUNCH GRASS: the dry, brittle, browned state of a lawn after weeks or months of summer drought

CURLYTOES: a visceral response to something disturbing or disgusting that prompts one's hands or feet to flex and twitch

DEER PATH: an apparent tunnel through the branches and underbrush of a forest created by wandering deer or perceptual patternicity

FAKE RAIN: downward-moving humidity that can be seen but barely felt. Specific to tropical coastal regions

FRIEND: any accidentally discovered or unearthed benign wild animal, bug, or occupied nest

GIANT-HOUSE-TINY-LOT SYNDROME: the suburban development trend of a grid of identical large, expensive houses with very small yards

GRAY SEASON: humid, rainy coastal winter months when weeks on end can pass without any visible sunlight, and seasonal affective disorder is rampant due to the relative lack of sunlight-created vitamin D

HABIQUAIL: an extension of the main quail pen consisting of a quail-sized PVC pipe tunnel leading to a second, smaller pen

MISSUS: an obviously pregnant or nursing female animal

NOODLE, NOODLING AROUND or ABOUT: to wander around a small area with no specific goal, often attending to minor, unplanned tasks as they are noticed

NOPE BUG: any spider or insect that is so large and intimidating or distasteful in appearance that instead of catching and eating it, a house cat will call over a human who doesn't want to deal with the bug either

NUCLEAR DANDELIONS: *Hypochaeris radicata*, commonly called cat's-ear or false dandelions. Dry, wiry, skinny-stemmed, pathetic excuses for dandelions that appear to have survived some genetic-altering accident

PIG GLASS: chunks of old, broken glass, generally found on a beach, that are round-edged and cloudy from years of being ground down by other rocks in the wild

PIGFACED SHITWARBLER: any wild bird that, instead of taking one seed at a time from a bowl of birdseed and retreating to a tree branch to eat it so other birds can access the bowl, sits in the bowl for a half hour at a time, stuffing their face and pooping, looking altogether like a sweat-pants-clothed couch potato digging into a bag of chips in front of a television

POLISHING THE FENCE: doing inconsequential or invented outdoor tasks for the purpose of covertly eavesdropping

ROGUE VEGETABLE: any identifiable garden plant that was not intentionally planted but instead grew from fertilizer compost

SPICY HIVE: a honey bee colony that is noticeably faster to anger and more defensive than other colonies in the same yard

SWEAT BEES: alarming, tickly bugs that creep down the skin of one's neck, shoulders, and back while one is wearing a beekeeping suit on a very hot day; distinguishable from stinging bees only in that they move exclusively downward, and if one tears one's suit off in fright, they become invisible (not to be confused with Halictidae bees, an actual species of bees that are attracted to sweat)

TREE RATS: squirrels

TWOLEGS or **TWOLEGGED MEATCREATURE:** a human, as perceived by an animal or insect

UNRAVELATION: during or shortly after a tragic or traumatic event or upheaval that makes one feel as though one's world were falling apart, a moment of profound insight and calm clarity

Acknowledgments

THIS BOOK TAKES place on the traditional, unceded territory of the Coast Salish People, specifically the Kwantlen, q̓ic̓әy̓ (Katzie), Matsqui, and Semiahmoo First Nations.

"Advice for a New Beekeeper" was originally published by the Canadian Broadcasting Corporation on the CBC Books website, September 8, 2022.

The image of a bee cluster behaving like a swirling galaxy in "Advice to a New Beekeeper" is from a conversation with Clara Efting, age five.

The idea of inventing monsters to justify a fear of the dark in "Schrödinger's Sting" is from Dylan Brody's story, "Leaps of Faith and Plummeting Terrors."

The book about a town under a lake mentioned in "Burying the Bones" is *When Is a Man* by Aaron Shepard (Victoria, BC: Brindle & Glass, 2014).

The description of religion, science, and magic in "Beyond Science" is from a conversation with Les Ellenor.

"Fawn" is based on "The Fawn" by Bryant Ross.

The comparison between the death rates of bee colonies and cattle herds in "Pandora's Boxes" is from a conversation with Paul van Westendorp.

"Once Upon a Holly Tree" first appeared in *Against Death: 35 Essays on Living*, edited by Elee Kraljii Gardiner (Vancouver, BC: Anvil Press, 2019).

The protagonist portrayed as a modern Snow White in "Once Upon a Holly Tree" was inspired by a comment made by Sara Spilchen.

I EXTEND MY GRATITUDE:

To the Greater Vancouver spoken word and arts community. I am endlessly grateful for the many writers and performers of East Vancouver who have inspired my writing for decades, and for the event organizers—Bonnie Nish, Graham Olds, Heather Haley, David "Kyprios" Coles, R.C. Weslowski, Sean McGarragle, Steve Duncan, Susan Mullen, T. Paul Ste. Marie, and many others—who have encouraged and facilitated my work by allowing me to share it on their stages. To the teachers and professors who applauded and guided my writing knowledge, especially James Bowlby, John Lent, Les Ellenor, and Tom Konyves.

To those who provided valuable information, insight, and feedback during the writing of this book: Aaron Shepard, Catherine Lemay, Cera Rivers, Chelsea Prince, Christine Turner, Daniela Elza, Dawna Rae Hicks, Elee Kraljii Gardiner, Graham Robertson, Griffin Tedeschini, Jenn Griffin, Jonathan Reed, Julie Parrell, Mikayla Cameron, Nicole Valyear, Nyla Bedard, Patricia Morrison, Paul van Westendorp, Sasha Van Wie, Shannon Hyde, Shannon Rayne, Tawahum Bige, Trina Loreen Ferguson, and Waubgeshig Rice.

To the organizations and individuals that have held me up and encouraged my work, including Canada Council for the Arts, CBC Books, CBC Radio, the Banff Center for Arts and Creativity, Samantha Haywood of Transatlantic Agency, and Jennifer Croll and the editorial team of Greystone Books.

To Bryant Ross for supporting and encouraging this project with heart and hands, for being a rock amidst the storms.

SOUNDTRACK

"PROLOGUE: STORM"—The Fugitives, "It Might Just Rain Like This For Days"

"ADVICE TO A NEW BEEKEEPER"—Devin Townsend, "Ki"

"ARIA"—Young Spirit, "Ugly, Broke, and Chubby"

"FENCES"—Faderhead, "Summer Rain"

"RUDE"—Echos, "King of Disappointment"

"STARFISHES"—Jess Hill, "A Common Bird"

"THREE GRAMS"—C. R. Avery, "Insufficient Funds of Love"

"SCHRÖDINGER'S STING"—Puscifer, "Conditions of My Parole"

"DINER"—Black Lab, "Tell Me Why"

"BILL"—Veda Hille, "The Trees"

"SUSTENANCE"—Dominique Fricot, "Seashore"

"A THRONE FOR YOUR HEAVEN"—Devon More, "Mount Pleasant"

"HIGH TEA WITH ROYALTY"—Porcelain and the Tramps, "King of the World"

"BURYING THE BONES"—Devin Townsend, "Jainism"

"THINGS I HAVE UNEARTHED WHILE DIGGING HOLES"—Amanda Palmer, "The Point of It All"

"BEYOND SCIENCE"—V. V. Brown, "Ghosts"

"FAWN"—Last Amanda, "Unforgettable"

"PANDORA'S BOXES"—Wumpscut, "Christfuck"

"CATCH"—The Pluviophiles, "Voracious"

"REARVIEW MIRROR"—Kyprios, "Better Miracle"

"HOUSEWARMING"—The Matinee, "Who Stoned the Roses"

"ONCE UPON A HOLLY TREE"—Dan Mangan, "Basket"

"FLEDGE"—Andrew Coombes, "Vann Einmana Hjarta"

"EPILOGUE: EXODUS"—Peter Gabriel, "Panopticom"